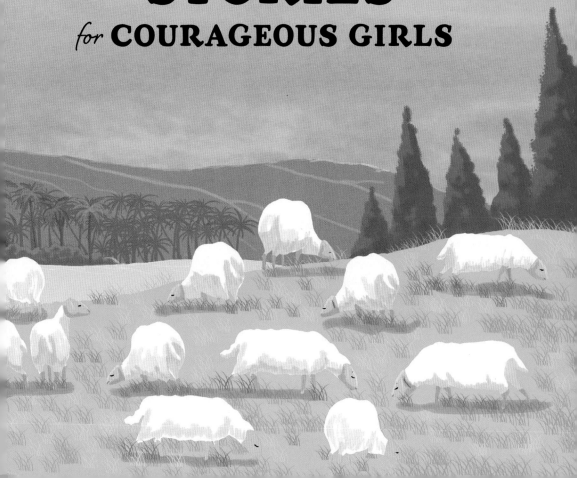

BIBLE
STORIES
for COURAGEOUS GIRLS

BIBLE
STORIES
for COURAGEOUS GIRLS

B&H KIDS

Nashville, Tennessee

Contents

Foreword

Dear Reader,

We're happy to introduce you to our first *Bible Stories for Courageous Girls*. It is our hope that this Bible storybook will not only introduce you to some of the most courageous people in history, but also inspire you to be a courageous believer too.

Being courageous is not about becoming someone great and important but is about sticking to the Way and continuing to believe in Jesus, even when some days are grey and indifferent. Being courageous is giving thanks and rejoicing in Him, even when there seems to be no reason to do so.

In this Bible storybook, you'll find the accounts of many ordinary women chosen by an extraordinary God. You will get to know the Bible characters a little better in each of their short introductions. These women trusted and obeyed God, and He gave them courage to act courageously in difficult situations. In the face of oppression, trials, and discouragements, these women succeeded and ultimately changed the course of their lives, their nation, and in some cases, even the course of history. This happened not because they were super heroes, but because the God in whom they trusted gave them courage and made them brave in spite of their fear and shortcomings.

God is still the same, and He still wants you to put your trust in Him in all situations. He will enable you to overcome trials and face challenges, as well as the dullness of your everyday life, with a courageous heart and mind.

We hope and pray that this *Bible Stories for Courageous Girls* will encourage and help you to live courageously.

"Since it is so likely that children will meet cruel enemies, let them at least have heard of brave knights and heroic courage. Otherwise you are making their destiny not brighter but darker."

—C.S. Lewis

8

The Old Testament

God Makes Heaven and Earth

Genesis 1:1-19

In the beginning, God created the heavens and the earth. The earth was a dark and empty place. There was only a roaring, black ocean covering empty land. The Spirit of God was hovering over the water. Then God said, "Let there be light!" Suddenly light shone down, and He created the first day.

On the second day, God said, "Let the water above be separated from the water on the earth." The waters obeyed God's command, and He called the expanse which separated the waters *sky*.

On the third day, God said, "Let the waters on the earth be separated by dry land. Let there be plants and trees on the land so that the earth may be filled with living things." Land appeared to separate the oceans, and trees spread their big leafy branches. Little flowers and plants sprung up out of the ground to greet the sun.

On the fourth day, God said, "Let the moon and stars shine at night, and let the sun shine by day. These lights will mark the seasons and shed light on the earth." God looked around and saw that all He had done was good.

God Makes the Creatures of the Ocean and the Sky

Genesis 1:20-23

On the fifth day, God said, "Let the ocean be filled with sea creatures!" Just then, the water began to churn with life. Great whales lifted their mighty heads. Dolphins jumped and splashed in the sunlight, and little sea crabs scuttled along the sea floor. God said, "Let the sky be filled with creatures of the air!" Seagulls swooped in the breeze along with butterflies and buzzing insects. God created all of them, big and small, and He saw that it was all good.

God Makes the Animals of the Earth
Genesis 1:24-25

"Now for the dry land," God said. "Let the deserts and valleys and mountains be filled with animals!" And that's what happened. The earth was filled with wild animals to roam the land and insects to creep along the ground.

God loved watching the animals play with each other. He was very pleased with His work.

EVE

- Mentioned in Genesis, 2 Corinthians, and 1 Timothy
- Meaning of name: Life—She was the very first woman and became the mother of the whole human race.
- She lived in: first inside Eden, but later outside of Eden
- Married to: Adam
- Mother of: Cain, Abel, Seth, and other sons and daughters

Milestones:

Eve did something she knew God had forbidden. Disobedience always has consequences. The first death occurred when Cain killed his brother Abel. God knew the risk of giving people free will to choose. But He promised to send a Savior, who would bear the consequence of our disobedience and defeat death.

Instead of confessing and asking for forgiveness, Eve blamed the serpent. Have you ever done something wrong and blamed someone else? How did you make it right? Can you think of a consequence for what happens when you have done wrong?

Adam named his wife Eve, because she would become the mother of all the living.
Genesis 3:20

Adam and Eve

Genesis 1:26-2:3, 7, 18-25

On the sixth day, God looked around at all the animals of the earth and the animals of the sea and sky, and God said, "I will create human beings to rule over the animals and the land. They will be special because I will make them in My likeness."

Then God took a handful of soil, and out of it He made Adam. God loved Adam. He even let Adam name all the animals. But God said, "It isn't good for Adam to be alone. I will make a partner for him."

So while Adam was asleep, God took one of Adam's ribs, and out of it He created the first woman. Adam loved her and called her Eve.

God gave Adam and Eve His blessing. He said, "The earth is filled with animals you may rule over and many good plants and fruits you may eat. Fill the earth with your children, and care for all the living creatures!"

God was happy with all that He had created. It was perfect. On the seventh day, He rested from all His work.

The Garden of Eden

Genesis 2:8-17

Adam and Eve lived in a garden called Eden. The Garden of Eden was a lush and colorful paradise.

God placed a tree called the Tree of Knowledge in the middle of the garden. God told Adam and Eve that they could eat from any of the trees in the garden except from the Tree of Knowledge. If they ate from it, God warned they would surely die.

Adam and Eve Disobey God

Genesis 3:1-7

One day the serpent slithered up to Eve as she was walking in the garden. "Why don't you take a bite from that juicy fruit hanging from the Tree of Knowledge?" he asked. Eve remembered what God had said. "God told us we must not eat fruit from that tree or even touch it," she replied. To this the serpent answered with lies, "That is only because the fruit will allow you to know the difference between right and wrong. God doesn't want you to be as wise as He is."

Eve became curious. "What would be the harm in one tiny bite?" she said to herself. So she picked a fruit and tasted it. Then she handed the fruit to Adam, and he also took a bite. When they looked at each other afterwards, they realized for the first time that they were naked. They were embarrassed and quickly sewed fig leaves together to cover themselves.

Out of Eden

Genesis 3:8-19

That day, Adam and Eve heard God walking in the Garden of Eden. They were frightened because they knew they had disobeyed Him. They hid behind the trees and plants, hoping God would not discover what they had done. But God knows all things.

God called out to Adam, "Where are you?" Adam came out from hiding and told God he was afraid because he was naked. God said, "How did you know you were naked? Did you eat the fruit I told you not to eat?"

Adam answered, "Eve was the one who took the fruit. It's her fault!" And Eve said, "But it was the snake who told me to take the fruit. So it's the snake's fault!"

God loved Adam and Eve, so He was very sad that they did not obey Him but chose to listen to the sneaky snake instead.

God gave Adam and Eve some animal skins to keep them warm. They had to leave the Garden of Eden. They had to live on dry land, work hard for their food, and they would eventually die.

NOAH'S WIFE

- Mentioned in Genesis
- We don't know her name. She must have been a very patient woman to put up with and support Noah's building project.
- She lived in: Mesopotamia, or modern day Iraq, before the flood, and in modern day Turkey after the flood
- Married to: Noah
- Mother of: Shem, Ham, and Japheth

Milestones:

Noah's wife, like her husband, had faith in God when nobody else did at the time. People probably thought they were crazy to build a huge boat far from the ocean. Together with her sons and their wives, she helped Noah in any way she could before, during, and after the Great Flood.

Questions:

Have you ever felt alone in your faith in God? Always remember Noah's wife standing by her husband and sons with faith, courage, and endurance.

And Noah and his sons and his wife and his sons' wives entered the ark to escape the waters of the flood.
Genesis 7:7

Noah Builds an Ark

Genesis 6:5-22

The world God made quickly filled with more and more people. God saw all their bad deeds. They cheated and stole and lied. God was sorry He had made them. So He decided to start over.

God planned a great flood. He would let rain pour down until it drenched the land and drowned the people. But there was one man God was pleased with. This man loved and obeyed God. His name was Noah.

God told Noah about His plan to flood the earth and put an end to all people except Noah's family. God gave Noah the plans to build a giant boat called an ark.

God said, "Make it big enough to hold you and your family as well as every kind of animal on earth."

Noah did just as God said. He and his sons worked hard hammering wood planks together and building the ark.

After many, many years, the ark was finally finished. Noah made sure to have a special place ready for each kind of animal. He packed the ark full of food and supplies.

The Great Flood

Genesis 7:1-17

Noah went into the ark with his wife, his three sons, and their wives. Then the animals marched inside. Two by two, the animals went into their stalls, and God closed the door to the ark. Then the windows of heaven were opened, and the rain came pouring down—first a sprinkle and then a torrent. The dry land was covered in water, and the ark began to float.

Forty Days and Forty Nights of Rain

Genesis 7:17–8:19

Rain poured down for forty days and forty nights. The flood was so deep that it covered the highest mountain peaks! Nothing on earth survived. Only Noah, his family, and the animals were saved. God was watching over them.

After it stopped raining, it still took many months for the water to disappear. One day Noah sent out a raven. The raven flew back and forth until the floodwaters had dried up.

Noah also sent out a dove. The dove came back unable to find a place of dry land anywhere. But when Noah sent the dove out again a week later, it returned with an olive leaf in its beak. The bird had found land!

"You can leave the ark now," God said to Noah. So Noah opened the door and called everybody out of the boat. Each of God's animals stepped off the boat, stretching their legs and sniffing the clean, fresh air. It must have felt good to walk on dry land after being penned up for so long in Noah's ark.

The Rainbow's Promise

Genesis 9:1-16

God gave a blessing to Noah and his family. He said to them, "May you have many children and grandchildren! Spread out all over the earth. It is yours. Take good care of it. I give you the plants and the animals for food. And I make a promise that I will keep forever: I will never again send a flood to destroy the earth."

Just then, the sun broke through the rain clouds. A beautiful rainbow full of bright colors shone in the sky. God said, "I have placed My rainbow in the clouds. It is the sign of My covenant with you and with all the earth. When I send rain over the earth, the rainbow will appear in the clouds, and I will remember My covenant with you and with all living creatures. Never again will the floodwaters destroy all life. This rainbow is the sign of My covenant."

SARAH

- Mentioned in Genesis, Isaiah, Romans, Hebrews, and 1 Peter
- Meaning of name: Her original name was Sarai, which means "princess." God changed her name to Sarah, which means "queen." This signified that Sarah was to be the mother of nations.
- She lived in: Ur of the Chaldees, Babylonia, which is modern day Iraq; Haran; Canaan; Egypt
- Married to: Abraham
- Mother of: Isaac

Milestones:

Sarah followed her husband on the long trek from Ur northward to Haran, then southward through Canaan to Egypt, and back to Canaan, where they eventually settled down. She became impatient waiting for the son God had promised and took things in her own hand, which caused a lot of problems. God, however, fulfilled His promise, and at long last Sarah gave birth to Isaac in her old age.

Sarah left her home with her family for a better life with God. Have you ever had to give something up or go through a change that was difficult and new? Have you found that God cares for you even when you mess up?

Sarah said, "God has brought me laughter, and everyone who hears about this will laugh with me." And she added, "Who would have said to Abraham that Sarah would nurse children? Yet I have borne him a son in his old age."
Genesis 21:6-7

God Chooses Abram

Genesis 12:1-9

Abram was one of God's special people. He lived in the city of Haran. One day God said to Abram, "Leave the place that you come from, and go to the land I will show you." Abram trusted God with his whole heart. He loaded his camels with all his belongings and left home with his wife, Sarai, his nephew Lot, and all their servants. They traveled through the desert hills with only God as their guide.

When Abram and his family came to the land of Canaan, God said, "This land is yours! It will belong to your family forever. I will bless you and all the people in your family who come after you. Everyone on earth will be blessed through you!" Abram felt very thankful so he built an altar in the desert where he could worship God. Then Abram and the rest of his group journeyed onward. Finally they came to a place they liked and pitched their tents and settled.

A Son for Abraham and Sarah

Genesis 17:1-18:15

One evening God said to Abram, "You will be the father of many nations. Look at the brilliant night sky! Can you count the stars? That is how many descendants you will have! No longer will you be called Abram. Your name will now be Abraham because you will be a father to many nations. And your wife's name will now be Sarah because you will have a son with her and kings will come from her." God had promised that Abraham and Sarah would have many descendants. However, Sarah was childless and too old to bear children. To solve the problem Sarah gave her slavegirl, Hagar, to Abraham as a second wife. Hagar gave birth to Ishmael. Now Abraham had a son.

One hot summer afternoon, Abraham was sitting outside his tent when three travelers came by. Abraham saw them and jumped up and called out to them, "Come, let me get you some water to wash your tired feet. And please come and rest a bit in the shade!" Then Abraham ran back to the tent. "Sarah!" he said, "Would you make some bread for our guests?" Sarah got cooking while Abraham went out in search of his best calf to serve with some milk and yogurt. The men gathered around under the shady trees sharing a drink and talking. Sarah was listening by the tent door.

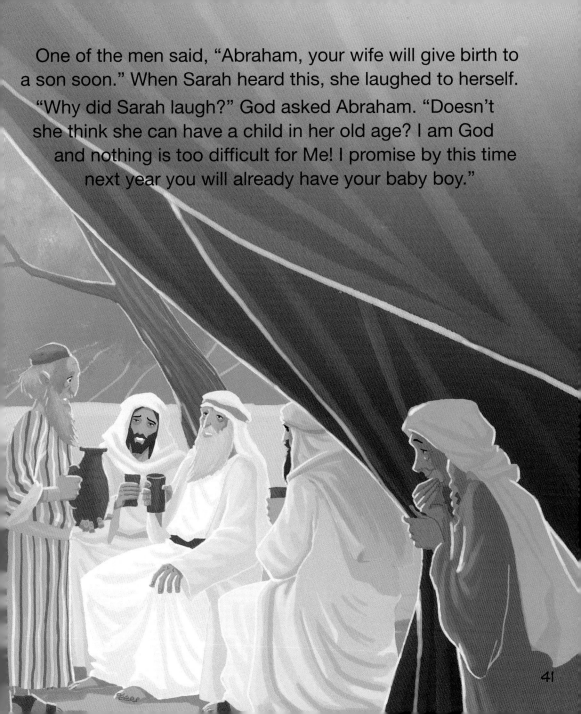

One of the men said, "Abraham, your wife will give birth to a son soon." When Sarah heard this, she laughed to herself.

"Why did Sarah laugh?" God asked Abraham. "Doesn't she think she can have a child in her old age? I am God and nothing is too difficult for Me! I promise by this time next year you will already have your baby boy."

Isaac Is Born

Genesis 21-22

God kept His promise to Abraham and Sarah. He gave them a healthy baby boy. They named him Isaac. Sarah looked up at her husband and said, "God has brought me laughter and everyone who hears will laugh with me! Who would have guessed that we would have a son in our old age?"

Now that she had Isaac, Sarah wasn't happy to have Hagar and Ishmael around, so she made Abraham send them away. Abraham was sad; Ishmael was his son afterall.

Sarah wasn't happy either when she heard God had asked Abraham to sacrifice Isaac to Him on a mountain. But Abraham trusted God and was ready to obey. At the last moment God said, "Stop!" and provided another sacrifice instead of Isaac.

Sarah was happy when Isaac returned home unharmed.

REBEKAH

- Mentioned in Genesis and Romans
- Meaning of name: Rebekah's name may refer to a rope or a team of cattle, but some think it means "a star" or "servant of God"
- Married to: Isaac, who was Abraham's son
- She lived in: Haran in modern day Turkey; later in Canaan, or modern day Israel
- Related to: She was a descendant of Nahor, Abraham's brother who came from Babylonia, which is in modern day Iraq.
- Mother of: Esau and Jacob

Milestones:

Rebekah was kind; she gave water to the camels. She was courageous to go with Abraham's servant to a land far away. She was clever in the way she handled the problems between Jacob and Esau. She was wise to send Jacob away to her brother, Laban, in Haran, when Esau was angry enough to kill him.

Questions:

Rebekah was kind to Abraham's servant when she gave him water and also watered his camels. How can you show kindness to people around you? How can you show extra kindness like Rachel did when she gave water to the man's camels?

So they called Rebekah and asked her, "Will you go with this man?" "I will go," she said.
Genesis 24:58

A Wife for Isaac

Genesis 24:1-27

Many years went by, and Sarah passed away. Abraham knew that soon he would be called up to heaven too. Before he died, he wanted to find a good wife for his son Isaac. Abraham called one of his most trusted servants to him and said, "Go to Haran where my brother Nahor lives. Find a good woman among his people for my son Isaac to marry."

When the servant arrived in Haran, he rested with his camels near a well where a young woman was filling her water jar.

"God of Abraham," prayed the servant. "I will ask the girl for a drink. If she offers to water my camels let it be the proof that she is the one You have chosen to be Isaac's wife."

The servant asked her for a drink. "I'll be glad to give you a drink," she answered. Then she saw the servant's thirsty camels and kindly offered them some water as well. "Thank you for your kindness," he told her. Then he asked, "Tell me, who is your family?" She replied, "My father is Bethuel, the son of Milkah and Nahor. My name is Rebekah." Abraham's servant asked Rebekah if he could stay with her family. "Yes, there is plenty of room," she said. Then the man bowed and worshiped the Lord. He had given Abraham, his master, success that day and led him to a wife for Isaac.

Isaac and Rebekah

Genesis 24:28-67

Abraham's servant told Rebekah's father why he had come. "I have been sent to find a wife for my master Abraham's son, Isaac, among his relatives. Rebekah has impressed me with her gentle kindness. I would like her to come back with me to be Isaac's wife!" Rebekah's brother and father said, "Let us ask the girl if she will go." When they asked her, she said, "I will!" Then they all knew that this was God's plan.

They blessed Rebekah and sent her with Abraham's servant.

Back in the land of Canaan, Isaac was walking out in his father's field when the servant and Rebekah approached on their camels. Rebekah spotted Isaac right away. "Who is that man walking toward us?" Rebekah asked. The servant replied, "That's Isaac— the man you will marry!" So Isaac and Rebekah were married, and they loved each other very much.

Jacob and Esau Are Born

Genesis 25:19-26; 27:1-45

Rebekah and Isaac wanted to have children, but God did not give them any. Isaac prayed to God to give them a child. Finally God answered his prayer. Rebekah became pregnant. She knew that she was pregnant with twins because she could feel them fighting with each other inside of her!

One day while Rebekah prayed, "Why is this happening to me?" God told her, "You will be blessed with two boys. But just like they are fighting inside of your womb, they will fight as they grow older too. They will separate into two different nations. The younger son will be strong and great. The older son will be his servant."

After nine long months of carrying the babies inside her, Rebekah gave birth. The first baby came out, and he was covered with bright red hair! They named him Esau. The second baby came out just behind, holding onto his brother's heel. They named him Jacob.

Rebekah loved Jacob most and helped him get his father's blessing. Then she sent him away to her brother in Harran.

51

Jacob Works for Laban

Genesis 29:1-14

Jacob's mother had sent him away from his angry brother, Esau, to go live with her brother, Laban. At last Jacob came to the land where his uncle lived. When he saw some shepherds by a well, he walked over to them and asked, "Do you know a man named Laban?"

"Yes, we do," they said. "And here comes his daughter Rachel with her sheep." The shepherds pointed to a girl who was heading toward the well. Jacob gave her some water for her sheep. He was so happy that he kissed her and started crying. He told her that he was the son of her aunt Rebekah. Rachel was amazed, and ran off to go and find her father.

When Laban heard about Jacob, he hurried to meet him. He kissed Jacob and said, "You are family. Stay here with us as long as you please." So Jacob stayed and lived with Laban and his family. He helped Laban by watching over his animals.

LEAH

- Mentioned in Genesis and Ruth
- Meaning of name: The name Leah could mean a few different things, but "weary, impatient" is one translation. Though she was Jacob's first wife, she was not his first choice, and was not as pretty as Rachel, her younger sister. But this did not stop her from being a devoted wife and mother.
- She lived in: Haran in modern day Turkey; later in Canaan, or modern day Israel
- Related to: Leah was the daughter of Laban, who was Rebekah's brother. Her sister was Rachel.
- Married to: Jacob
- Mother of: Reuben, Simeon, Levi, Judah, Issachar, Zebulun, and Dinah

Milestones:

Leah was a very loyal and good mother. While she had a troubled early life, she was blessed later after marrying Jacob. She had six sons and a daughter, Dinah. She praised the Lord for giving her so much.

Questions:

Leah was jealous of her younger sister's beauty and Jacob's love for her, but throughout her life, her attitude changed into loving herself for who she was and what she did. Have you ever been jeolous of someone or wanted their things or lifestyle? Often we must be reminded to praise God for what He's given us, which is our unique gift to the world.

When the L ORD saw that Leah was not loved, he enabled her to conceive, but Rachel remained childless.
Genesis 29:31

Leah & Rachel
RACHEL

- Mentioned in Genesis, Ruth, 1 Samuel, Jeremiah, and Matthew
- Meaning of name: Rachel means "Ewe," which is a female sheep. This was a form of endearment, like calling someone sweetie or dear.
- She lived in: Haran in modern day Turkey; later in Canaan, or modern day Israel
- Related to: Rachel was the daughter of Laban, who was Rebekah's brother. Her sister was Leah.
- Married to: Jacob
- Mother of: Joseph and Benjamin

Milestones:

Rachel endured many years of being childless, which was shameful in Biblical times. Although Jacob loved Rachel very much, she was jealous of her sister, Leah, who had many children. She was very thankful when God finally gave her Joseph, her first child.

Questions:

Rachel had to wait many years for an answer to her prayers. Have you ever had to wait for something you really wanted? How can you wait patiently for something?

Jacob was in love with Rachel and said, "I'll work for you seven years in return for your younger daughter Rachel."
Genesis 29:18

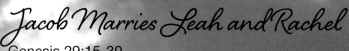

Jacob Marries Leah and Rachel

Genesis 29:15-30

Rachel was very beautiful, and Jacob had fallen in love with her. One day Laban said to Jacob, "It isn't right for you to work without pay. What can I give you in return?" Jacob told Laban, "If you let me marry Rachel, I will work seven years for you." So Laban and Jacob made an agreement. Jacob worked seven years for Laban. The time did not seem very long for Jacob because he was so in love with Rachel.

At last the day came for the wedding. Laban prepared a big feast with lots of friends and family. But when Laban brought out the bride, it was Leah, and not Rachel.

Jacob panicked. He turned to Laban and said, "Where's Rachel? I worked seven years for her, not Leah!"

Laban told him, "In our country the older daughter must marry first. You can marry Rachel. But you'll have to work seven more years for me." So Jacob married Rachel, too. But he had to work seven more years for Laban after they were married.

Jacob Becomes Rich

Genesis 30:25-43

Jacob worked many years for Laban. But he had many children with his wives, and he was eager to start his own life. "Please let me go," he said to Laban. "You know, I've worked for you long enough, and I want to go back to my homeland."

"My dear Jacob," Laban replied. "Please stay and I will give you anything you ask." Jacob did not want to stay, so he came up with a plan. "Alright," he said. "Give me all your sheep and goats that are either spotted or speckled." Laban agreed but cheated Jacob by removing those animals and sending them far away to be looked after by his sons.

Meanwhile Jacob also cheated Laban. He peeled strips of bark off tree branches so they looked speckled. Then he placed them

around the drinking place. Jacob made sure that the best animals could see the branches. Their babies were born with spots all over them. They were also healthy and strong. Jacob kept these spotted and speckled sheep and goats and made a lot of money off of them. He became rich and bought more sheep and goats. Then he had enough money to buy camels and donkeys and servants.

MIRIAM

- Mentioned in: Exodus, Numbers, Deuteronomy, and Micah
- Meaning of name: Wished-for child, rebellious, strong waters, or beloved
- She lived in: Egypt and Sinai
- Related to: Moses and Aaron

Milestones:

Miriam helped save the life of her younger brother, Moses. She also helped the Hebrew people escape from Egypt under Moses' leadership.

Miriam is known as a prophetess and poet: She helped compose, along with Moses, a beautiful song after God saved Israel from the Egyptians. With the Red Sea closing, Miriam and Moses sang the glorious song to God. Have you ever been inspired to write a song or create something that praises God?

Then Miriam the prophet, Aaron's sister, took a timbrel in her hand, and all the women followed her, with timbrels and dancing. Miriam sang to them: "Sing to the LORD, for he is highly exalted. Both horse and driver he has hurled into the sea."
Exodus 15:20-21

Moses Is Born

Exodus 2:1-4

During this time there was a man and a woman from the Hebrew tribe of Levi living in Egypt. The woman had just given birth to a baby boy. When she heard the king's order, she panicked. She loved her baby; he was her pride and joy. So she searched her house and found a spot where she could hide him and kept him hidden for three months. During this time the king's officials were roaming the country.

They were killing every baby boy that belonged to the Hebrews. The woman decided she had to find a better hiding spot. So she took a basket made of papyrus reeds and made it waterproof with tar. She put her baby in the basket. Then she sneaked down to the riverbank, and she let the basket float among the reeds in the water. Miriam, the baby's older sister, had followed her mother down to the river. Her mother went back home, but Miriam stayed crouching down in the grass. She wanted to watch over her brother and see what would happen to him.

Saved by a Princess

Exodus 2:5-10

While Miriam was watching her brother, the king's daughter came down to the river to bathe. As she approached the riverbank, she saw something floating on the water. She told her servant to wade into the river and fetch whatever was floating in it. They were surprised to find a basket with a little baby boy inside.

The princess immediately picked up the baby and rocked him gently. Miriam hurried over and said, "Princess, I see that you love this little baby. Perhaps I can find a woman to care for him until he is old enough for you to keep."

The princess smiled at Miriam. "Yes, that's a fine idea," she said. So Miriam took her little brother back to their mother to nurse him until he was old enough to be adopted. She then took him to the princess, who named him Moses.

Moses Stands Up for a Slave

Exodus 2:11-15

Moses grew up in the palace. He was treated like a prince and had the best of everything, plenty to eat, and the finest clothes. One day Moses took a walk outside of the palace grounds. He saw the Hebrews, his people, slaving away under the hot sun. Then he noticed that one of them was being beaten by an Egyptian slave master.

Moses was furious and ran over to save the man who was being beaten. He grabbed the slave master with both hands and killed him. Moses hid the body in the sand, but someone found out about what he had done. Everybody began to gossip about Moses. The king heard and was so angry that he sent his men to arrest Moses and have him killed. Moses had to run away. He did not stop until he crossed the border and reached the land of Midian in the desert.

Jethro Welcomes Moses

Exodus 2:14-21

Once Moses arrived in Midian, he sat down by a well and had a drink of water. Just then, the seven daughters of a priest named Jethro came to the well to give water to their sheep and goats. But a group of shepherds tried to bully them. Moses stood up for the girls and chased the shepherds away. Then Moses offered to water the women's sheep and goats himself. They thanked him and went back to their father's house.

"Why do you come so early today?" their father asked when they came in. The women told him about the shepherds who bullied them. "But a young

Hebrew helped us," they explained. "And he even watered our flocks."

"Why didn't you invite him to our home?" Jethro replied. "We must return his kindness and let him stay with us."

The girls went back to find Moses. They invited him to come and live with them. So Moses stayed with Jethro, and eventually married one of his daughters, named Zipporah.

The Burning Bush

Exodus 3:1-10

One day Moses was guarding Jethro's sheep and goats on the mountainside. He was wandering along the trail when, suddenly, something incredible happened. He saw a bush light up in flames. As he stepped closer to get a better look, he noticed that the bush was not burning up. Then the voice of God called to Moses from the bush,"Moses! Don't come any closer. Take your shoes off, for this is holy ground. I am the God of Abraham, Isaac, and Jacob." Now Moses covered his face for he was afraid to see God.

"Moses, I am here to tell you that I have not forgotten My beloved people. I know that they are suffering as slaves in Egypt. I have heard their cries, and I will answer their prayers. I have something special in store for them. I have chosen you, Moses, to lead My people out of Egypt. You will bring them safely to the land I have promised your ancestors."

Ten Plagues

Exodus 7:14-11:10; 12:29-32

Moses and his brother Aaron went to see the king of Egypt.
The king, Pharaoh, did not want to let the Hebrew people go.
Because Pharaoh did not obey, God inflicted plagues upon
Pharaoh and Egypt.

First God turned the Nile River into blood. But Pharaoh did not
let the Israelites go. God brought thousands of frogs to Egypt.
But still Pharaoh refused God's order. God brought
gnats, flies, and allowed Egypt's livestock to
die from disease. Still Pharaoh refused.

God brought boils and a thunderstorm of hail and locusts that ate everything growing in the fields, but still Pharaoh's heart was hardened. Pharaoh said "no." God darkened the sky, even during the day, and still, Pharaoh was stubborn.

God told Moses that He would bring a final, tenth plague upon Egypt: "I will strike down the firstborn of both people and cattle," God said. But God promised not to kill the Israelites' firstborn if they painted lamb's blood above their doors. So it happened that all the firstborn were struck down except the Israelites. Pharaoh finally recognized God's power and told Moses to leave with his people.

The Exodus

Exodus 13:17-14:4

God led His people through the deserts of Egypt. He never left them. During the day He appeared as a cloud leading the way before them. At night He lit up their path in the form of a pillar of fire. The people walked a long way, and when they came to a place called Etham near the border, they needed to rest. They set up camp and spent the night there. The next day God told them to camp in a different spot. He knew the king and His army would chase after Israel. He was going to show his great power and help the Israelites win. The people obeyed and camped where God led them. Then they pitched their tents, tied up their animals, and went to sleep.

The King's Chase

Exodus 14:5-14

The king of Egypt was told that the Hebrews had fled. "Look what we've done!" he shouted to his men. "We let them go, and now we'll have no slaves." Six hundred horse-drawn chariots were loaded with soldiers. The king led them on a chase to recapture the Israelite people.

When the Israelites saw the chariots heading toward them from afar, they were frightened and ran to Moses. "You brought us out of slavery only to die here in the desert," they moaned, "and now the king will kill us all!" But Moses knew that the Lord had a plan. "Don't be afraid," he said. "You will see God work His miracles. Have faith! God will take care of us."

The Parting of the Red Sea

Exodus 14:15-31

God told Moses, "Tell the people to start heading toward the Red Sea. When you get to the water, hold your hand out. I will part the waters, and you will be able to march across to the other side." So Moses led the people toward the sea. As they approached the shore, Moses held his hand out. All night a strong east wind drove the sea back and turned it into dry land. Now Israel could cross the Red Sea. The Egyptian army was amazed. They followed right behind in their chariots.

Once all the Israelite people had safely crossed over, Moses held his hand above the water, and the waves crashed together again. The Egyptian army drowned with their chariots in the wild, foamy waves. When the Israelites saw how God saved them, they respected God and returned to their faith in Him and His servant Moses.

Water for the Thirsty

Exodus 15:1-27

The Israelites celebrated their victory. The Lord had saved them! They sang out, "Praise the Lord for His great victory! He has thrown the horses and their riders into the sea." Moses' sister Miriam shook her tambourine and began to dance and sing. The other women joined in and praised the Lord with their songs.

After that, Moses led the people into the Shur Desert. They walked for three days without water. The people were tired and thirsty.

Finally, they found some water at a place called Marah. But as soon as they took a drink, they spit it out again. The water tasted bitter. "What are we going to drink?" they asked Moses. But Moses didn't know, so he prayed. God told Moses to throw a piece of wood into the water. Moses obeyed, and the water turned clean and fresh. The people drank as much as they could. Then they filled up their casks and walked on.

Later on, they came to an oasis with twelve springs and seventy palm trees. They stopped there and camped for some time.

Food for the Hungry

Exodus 16:1-20

The people walked through the desert a long time on their way to Mount Sinai. The sun beat down on them, and they were quickly running out of food. They began to complain, wishing they had stayed in Egypt because at least there they would have food.

God spoke to Moses and said, "I have heard My people cry. Tell them I will send food from heaven. Then they will know I am God, and they will trust in Me."

That evening, a flock of quail landed among their tents. The people roasted the birds and ate the delicious meat. Then they went to sleep. When they peeked out of their tents the next morning, they saw the ground was covered with little white flakes. "What is this?" they asked. Moses answered, "This is the bread God has given us to eat today." The people called the bread Manna. It tasted like sweet wafers made with honey. The people gathered up the Manna bread and ate until they were full.

The Ten Commandments

Exodus 19:16-20:17; 24:12

When the Israelites reached Mount Sinai, they camped there for some time. God told Moses to climb the mountain and meet Him there. Moses reached the top, and God spoke to him from the blazing fire. "I am God, the One who has brought you out of slavery in Egypt," He said. "These are My Ten Commandments:

Do not worship any God but Me.

Do not worship idols and false images.

Do not swear and misuse My name.

Remember the seventh day—the Sabbath, and keep it holy.

Respect your father and mother.

Do not murder.

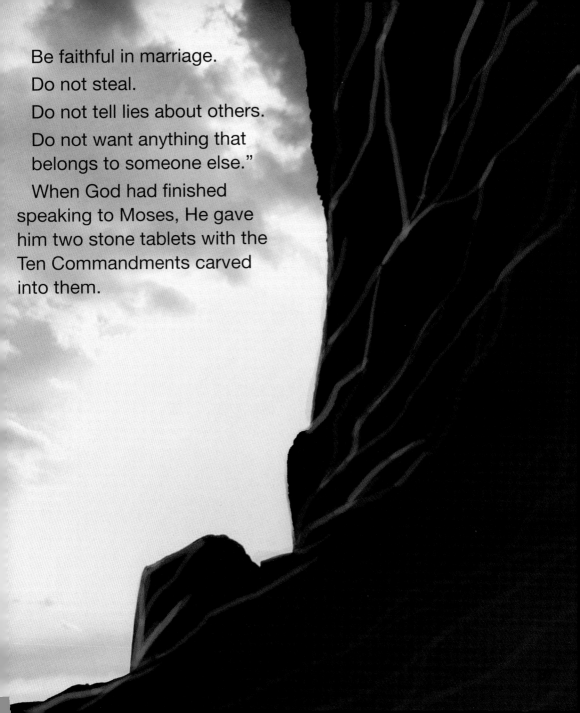

Be faithful in marriage.
Do not steal.
Do not tell lies about others.
Do not want anything that
belongs to someone else."

When God had finished
speaking to Moses, He gave
him two stone tablets with the
Ten Commandments carved
into them.

Joshua Becomes the Leader of Israel

Joshua 1:1-9

When the Israelites finally reached the border of the Promised Land, Moses died. Aaron and Miriam had also died. Who would lead the Israelites into the land? Then God spoke to Joshua, who had been Moses' special helper. "Now that Moses is gone, you must lead the people across the Jordan River into the Promised Land. Wherever you go, I will give you that land. I will be with you, just as I was with Moses. Be strong and courageous. Remember what Moses taught you. Read the Book of Law and obey my words. Do not be afraid or discouraged. The LORD your God will be with you wherever you go." So Joshua become the new leader of Israel.

RAHAB

- Mentioned in: Joshua, Matthew, Hebrews, and James
- Meaning of name: Generous
- She lived in: Jericho (one of the oldest cities in the world) in ancient Israel, which is the modern day West Bank
- Related to: In the genealogy of Jesus, we discover that Rahab became the wife of Salmon, one of the Israelite spies she had helped.

Milestones:

Rahab didn't just stand and let things happen. She did something. She knew, that the Israelites would take Jericho, so in order to save her family, she helped the two Israelite spies escape the king's soldiers.

Questions:

Rahab risked her life to save the spies so that they could save her family. Do you know of someone that has performed such a courageous act of faith?

So the young men who had done the spying went in and brought out Rahab, her father and mother, her brothers and sisters and all who belonged to her. They brought out her entire family and put them in a place outside the camp of Israel.

Joshua 6:23

Rahab Helps the Spies

Joshua 2:1-7

Joshua sent two spies into Canaan to the town of Jericho. They met a woman there named Rahab. She let the spies stay in her home, but some men found out about them. "Some Israelites have come to spy on us," they told the king of Jericho. "They are staying in Rahab's home."

So the king ordered his soldiers to go and arrest the men. The soldiers found Rahab's house and knocked on her front door, but Rahab had been clever and covered the spies up underneath some leafy plants on her roof. Then she went and opened her door.

The soldiers said, "Where are the spies you've been hiding? We have come to arrest them."

"They were here," Rahab replied, "but they left already. If you hurry you may be able to catch them."

So the soldiers went away and searched the road near the Jordan River.

Rahab Asks a Favor

Joshua 2:8-14

Meanwhile back in Jericho, Rahab told the spies, "The soldiers are gone! You can come out now." Then she told them, "I know that God has given Israel this land. He rules the heaven and earth.

Everyone in Jericho has heard how God parted the Red Sea. And everyone knows that God led your people out of Egypt. Now they shake with fear because you are coming. But when the day comes for you to take Jericho, please remember my family. Treat them with the same kindness that I have treated you."

The spies replied, "If you keep quiet, we will do as you have asked. We won't harm your family, and may God punish us if we don't keep our promise."

The Spies Escape

Joshua 2:15-24

Rahab's home was part of the city wall, so she tied a red rope to her upper window that ran all the way down to the ground below. She told the two spies, "Use this rope to lower yourselves down. You must leave quietly and then go hide in the hills. The king's soldiers won't find you there. They'll give up and come back to Jericho. Then you'll be safe."

The spies thanked Rahab and said to her, "When our people take Jericho, leave this red rope hanging in your window. Then we will remember not to harm you or your family inside." Rahab agreed.

The spies lowered themselves down the rope and left Jericho. They hid in the hills for three days, and the soldiers never found them. When the spies returned to the camp, they told Joshua and the Israelites everything that had happened. "The people of Jericho are frightened," the spies said. "They know the Lord is with us!"

DEBORAH

- Mentioned in: Judges
- Meaning of name: Bee
- She lived in: Canaan, or modern day Israel
- Married to: Lapidoth

Milestones:

Deborah was an unusual woman for her time. She is the only female Hebrew judge listed in the Bible. She is known as the "mother of Israel" because of her wise decisions in times of both peace and war.

Can you name a woman like Deborah who was the first of her kind? The first female astronaut? The first female Nobel Prize winner?

Then Deborah said to Barak, "Go! This is the day the LORD has given Sisera into your hands. Has not the LORD gone ahead of you?" So Barak went down Mount Tabor, with ten thousand men following him.
Judges 4:14

Deborah and Barak

Judges 4:1-16

After they settled in the Promised Land, the Israelites started to sin again. Then the Lord let the Canaanite king named Jabin capture Israel. Jabin had a great army. The leader of the army was a man named Sisera. He was tough and cruel to the Israelites. The people prayed for God's help.

At this time, Deborah was the leader of Israel. Every day Deborah sat under a palm tree. The people came to her with their disputes, and she would help them. The Lord had given her wisdom. She was a prophet of God, and sometimes God spoke to her and told her what to do.

One day Deborah received a message from God. She sent for a man named Barak to meet her under the palm tree. She said, "Barak, I have a message for you from God. Gather an army of ten thousand people and lead them to Mount Tabor. The Lord is going to help you defeat the Canaanites. God will lead Sisera and his troops to the Kishon River and will give him into your hands."

Barak said, "I will only go if you go, too."

"Alright, I'll go," said Deborah, "But because you want to do it that way, the Lord is going to let a woman win against Sisera instead of you."

Then Barak and Deborah left to gather the troops.

The Lord Fights for Israel

Judges 4:10-24

Deborah and Barak led their army toward Mount Tabor. Sisera got word that Israel was preparing for battle. "Let's go," he called out to his soldiers. "The Israelites think they're going to beat us today!" The soldiers laughed and made fun of Israel as they climbed into their iron chariots.

Meanwhile, Deborah told Barak, "The Lord has already gone on ahead to fight for us!" Barak led the troops down the mountain. Sisera and his army were waiting below. During the battle, the Lord fought for Israel. He confused Sisera's army and made them afraid.

They began to jump off their chariots and run away. Even Sisera tried to run away, but Barak's army ran after them. Before Barak could catch up to Sisera, a woman who lived nearby killed Sisera herself. She took Barak to her tent and showed him that Sisera was dead. Because God gave them the victory, the Canaanites no longer had any power over Israel. That day Deborah and Barak sang, "Our Lord, we pray that all Your enemies will die like Sisera. But let everyone who loves You shine brightly like the rising sun."

After that, Israel lived in peace for about forty years.

Ruth & Naomi
RUTH

- Mentioned in: The Book of Ruth and Matthew
- Meaning of name: Friend
- She lived in: Moab and Bethlehem
- Related to: Naomi, her mother-in-law
- Mother of: Obed

Milestones:

Ruth was a real friend, the very best friend a person could ever have. She was a friend to her mother-in-law, Naomi, and a friend to God. Ruth is one of the greatest examples of a person who sticks with both God and their friends through thick and thin, no matter what. She is also an example of someone who recognizes the might and power of God.

Questions:

Were you ever disappointed by a friend? Were you ever helped by a friend who came through when you least expected it? What can you do to become a friend like Ruth to your friends?

But Ruth replied, "Don't urge me to leave you or to turn back from you. Where you go I will go, and where you stay I will stay. Your people will be my people and your God my God.
Ruth 1:16

Ruth & Naomi
NAOMI

- Mentioned in: The Book of Ruth
- Meaning of name: Naomi means "pleasant." For a while she called herself Mara, meaning "bitter."
- She lived in: Judah and Moab and then Judah again
- Related to: Naomi was Ruth's mother-in-law
- Mother of: Malon and Kilion

Milestones:

Though Naomi had gone through many hardships while away from the Promised Land, she endured. Going back with Ruth, she found peace in the land of God. She encouraged Ruth to find love again, and for herself, found peace with God after being away so long.

When we grow far from God, we feel empty. Have you felt far from God? Do you know that you can always come back, like Naomi?

The women said to Naomi: "Praise be to the LORD, who this day has not left you without a guardian-redeemer. May he become famous throughout Israel! _Ruth 4:14_

Ruth Is Loyal to Naomi

Ruth 1:1-19

Once there was a famine in the land of Judah.
A woman named Naomi and her husband and
two sons moved to Moab where there was food.
Naomi's husband died, but her sons grew up and
married Moabite women named Orpah and Ruth.

Some time later, the two sons died, and Naomi
decided to go back to the land
of Judah.

On the way, Naomi said to her daughters-in-law, "Why don't you go back to your own mothers? You've been with me long enough." But the women would not go.

"We want to be with you," they said.

"But what good am I to you?" Naomi asked them. "I have no more sons to give you to be your husbands."

So Orpah went back to her family, but Ruth stayed with Naomi. Ruth told Naomi, "You are my family, and I will not leave you alone. Where you go, I will go. Your people will be my people. And your God will be my God."

Then they traveled on until they reached the town of Bethlehem, where Naomi had lived ten years earlier. All her old friends and family still lived there. When they saw her, they said, "Can this be our old friend Naomi?"

Ruth Meets Boaz

Ruth 2:1-23

Ruth told Naomi, "Why don't you rest. I'll go see if I can find us some food." So Ruth walked out into the fields where the men were harvesting. The field was owned by a man named Boaz. He was one of Naomi's relatives. He was a rich and important man, but he was also kind and gentle.

When he saw Ruth wandering in his fields, he asked his workers who she was.

"That's Naomi's daughter-in-law," they answered. "She wants to gather the leftovers from our field." So Boaz walked over to Ruth and smiled. "You're welcome to pick up whatever is left over in my field," he told her. "I told the men not to bother you. And be sure to drink from the water jar whenever you're thirsty." Ruth bowed down and asked, "Why are you being so kind to me?" "Because you have been good to my relative Naomi," he said. "I have heard how you left your home and your family to be with Naomi. I pray the Lord will reward you."

So Ruth worked in the fields all day. When she returned to Naomi, she gave her the food she had gleaned. "Daughter, you picked all of this from Boaz's field?" Naomi exclaimed. "May the Lord bless him!"

Boaz let Ruth pick the wheat and barley in his fields until the harvest was over.

Ruth and Boaz Get Married

Ruth 3:1-4:17

One day Naomi said to Ruth, "You're still young, and Boaz has been so good to us. He sleeps in the field tonight. Why don't you go and lie down at his feet. Then he will see that you would like to be his wife."

So Ruth picked out her nicest clothes and put on some perfume. Boaz ate and drank his food, then went to sleep. Then Ruth lifted the corner of the blanket near his feet and lay down. Boaz didn't wake up until the middle of the night. He felt someone moving near his feet. "Who's there?" he said.

"It's Ruth," she answered.

Boaz said, "Ruth, you are such a lovely woman. Any young man would marry you. But you have come to me, and that shows you are loyal to your family."

Boaz married Ruth and the whole town gave them their blessing. Ruth became pregnant with a son. She named him Obed. Naomi was a very proud grandma. She would spend hours bouncing the baby on her lap. The townspeople began to call him "Naomi's Boy."

When Obed grew up, he had a son named Jesse. And Jesse's youngest son was David—the king of Israel. So Naomi became the great-great grandmother of a king!

HANNAH

- Mentioned in: 1 Samuel
- Meaning of name: Gracious
- She lived in: Ancient Israel
- Married to: Elkanah
- Mother of: Samuel, three other sons and two daughters

Milestones:

Hannah couldn't have children, so she prayed to God that she might be blessed with a child. After Samuel was born, she kept her promise to give him to God, though she must have missed him very much.

Questions:

Have you ever humbled yourself before God? Have you ever wanted something so badly, but knew you had to have faith in God in order to achieve it?

So in the course of time Hannah became pregnant and gave birth to a son. She named him Samuel, saying, "Because I asked the LORD for him."
1 Samuel 1:20

Hannah Asks the Lord for a Child

1 Samuel 1:1-17

Hannah was a godly woman. She had a husband named Elkanah. He also had another wife named Peninnah who had many children. Hannah had none. Hannah wanted a child more than anything in the world. Elkanah loved Hannah more than Peninnah and felt bad that she didn't have any children.

One day Elkanah took a trip with his family to worship the Lord at Shiloh. He sacrificed an animal to God. Then he gave his wives and children some of the meat. Because he loved Hannah and felt sorry she had no children, he always gave her the biggest piece. Peninnah was jealous and made fun of Hannah, saying, "It's too bad the Lord won't give you any children." Hannah cried and went to the Lord's house to pray: "Lord, You have given me so much. But I am so sad. Please let me have a son. I promise he will be Yours until the day he dies." Eli, the priest, saw Hannah's lips moving, but no words came out. Her prayer was deep inside her heart. Eli told Hannah, "Go home now, and may God grant you whatever you were praying for."

Samuel Is Born

1 Samuel 1:19-28; 2:18-21

God answered Hannah's prayer. She gave birth to a son, and she named him Samuel. When Samuel was just a toddler, Hannah brought him to the Lord's house at Shiloh. She found Eli the priest and told him, "A few years ago I stood here and prayed for a son. You told me that the Lord would answer my prayer, and He did!"

Samuel peaked out behind his mother's skirt and looked up shyly at Eli. Then Hannah said, "I am giving him over to you so that he can grow up in the Lord's house."

Eli agreed to keep Samuel with him at Shiloh. He was like a father toward Samuel, and he taught him about the Lord. Once a year, Samuel's mother and father came to visit. Hannah always brought Samuel new clothes to wear. Eli knew how much they loved their son. He blessed Hannah and Elkanah and told them, "I pray that the Lord will bless you with more children!"

God was good to Hannah. He gave her three more sons and two daughters.

God Calls Samuel

1 Samuel 3:2-18

Eli the priest had two sons. But his sons didn't care about God. So Samuel became Eli's closest companion. One night after they both had gone to bed, Samuel heard someone call his name. He ran to Eli's room and said, "Here I am." But Eli said, "I didn't call for you. Go back to bed." So Samuel went back and tried to go to sleep. But again the voice called, "Samuel!" Samuel went to Eli again, "Here I am. I heard you call me." "No son," said Eli. "I didn't call you. Go back to bed."

Once Samuel laid back down, the voice called to him a third time, "Samuel!" Samuel went to Eli's room again, "Here I am. I heard you call me." By this time Eli realized the voice was God calling to Samuel. He told Samuel, "When you hear the voice call you again, say, 'Here I am, Lord. I am listening.'" Samuel went back to bed. And the Lord called, "Samuel!" Then Samuel said, "Here I am, Lord. I am listening." And the Lord said, "I have warned Eli that his sons were sinning. But he has not listened to me. Now I have no choice but to punish him and his family for their sins."

The next morning, Samuel told Eli everything. Eli was sad, but said, "He is the Lord. He will do what is right."

David and Saul

1 Samuel 16:14-23

Many years later, God had chosen Saul to be the first king of Israel. But after some years Saul no longer obeyed God's commands, and God's Spirit left him. Because God was no longer with Saul, he had been taken over by an evil spirit that would not give him peace. At night Saul often awoke with horrible nightmares. During the day he wrestled with bad thoughts.

One day when Saul was feeling particularly bad, his servants sent for a musician to come and play to calm him down.

David was still a young man, but he played the harp very well. Saul's servants heard good things about David, so they hired him to play the harp for Saul. When David plucked the strings of his instrument, a peaceful melody filled the air. His music seemed to come from heaven. Saul immediately relaxed, and the bad spirit left him. Saul loved David very much. But sometimes he was so angry and jealous that he tried to kill him.

ABIGAIL

- Mentioned in: 1 Samuel
- Meaning of name: Joyful
- She lived in: Carmel in ancient Israel
- Married to: King David
- Mother of: Several children

Milestones:

She intervened between David and her first husband, a brute of a man named Nabal. Through her devotion and wisdom, she stopped David from interfering with God's will.

Do you think that a soft, peaceful voice can calm anger, like Abigail calmed David? How can you talk to someone who has become angry?

David said to Abigail, *"Praise be to the L*ORD*, the God of Israel, who has sent you today to meet me. May you be blessed for your good judgment and for keeping me from bloodshed this day and from avenging myself with my own hands."*
1 Samuel 25:32-33

David and Nabal

1 Samuel 25:2-13

When Samuel grew up and became God's prophet, he anointed Saul as king over Israel, but because Saul did not obey God, God told Samuel to anoint David who would become the new king after Saul. Soon Saul began to hate David for being chosen as the new king and decided to kill him. David ran away to the desert.

David and his men were kind to the shepherds in these lands, helping them to protect their flocks. One day, David and his men ran out of food. David sent ten men to a man named Nabal, a wealthy landowner in charge of many flocks. Even though David and his men had been kind to Nabal's shepherds, Nabal was gruff and mean. "Why should I give you my food? David is just a runaway."

When his men returned and told him, David was furious. He clenched his fists in anger and said, "Get your swords!" David strapped his sword on, too, and took four hundred of his men and started out to Nabal's land.

Abigail Makes Peace

1 Samuel 25:14-31

Abigail was Nabal's wife. She had heard that her husband had not been kind to David. She was sorry, but she was also worried that David would take his revenge out on Nabal and their family. She left at once to apologize and offer David the food he had asked for. Abigail rode as fast as she could to meet David. Behind her were several donkeys carrying heavy sacks on their backs. The sacks were overflowing with wine, meat, raisins, bread, and all kinds of good things to eat and drink.

When Abigail saw David, she fell down on her knees. "My husband is foolish," she cried out. "He does not realize that God has promised to make you the ruler of Israel! Please forgive him and do not harm us. You have never killed innocent people before because you are good and God is with you. Let this gift be given to the men who follow you."

David and Abigail

1 Samuel 25:32-42

After David heard what Abigail had to say, he smiled. "Praise the Lord who has sent you to meet me," David told her. "I was about to attack your husband's household. You should be praised. You have saved your family and have kept me from seeking revenge. Abigail, go home now. Don't worry. We will not harm you or your husband!" So Abigail thanked David and went home.

When she got home, Abigail found her husband Nabal stuffing his mouth full of food, laughing and drinking, and acting foolish with all his friends. Abigail waited until the morning when her husband was sober. Then she told Nabal that David had planned to attack him until she had gone to make peace. Nabal was so surprised that he had a heart attack. Ten days later, he died. David heard the news and said, "Praise be to the Lord! I did not have to kill Nabal. Nabal killed himself with his own foolish behavior."

Then David sent a message to Abigail asking her to marry him. Abigail rode away with his messengers to David and became his wife.

God Will Provide

1 Kings 17:8-16

During a long famine in Israel, God told his prophet Elijah, "Go to the town of Zarephath. There's a widow living there. She will give you some food." So Elijah walked until he came to the town gates. He saw a widow gathering sticks for a fire.

"Would you give me a drink of water?" he asked her. And so the widow brought him some water.

Then he asked her, "Is there a piece of bread I might have too?" The widow answered, "I don't have any bread. I only have some flour and some olive oil. I was going home to build a fire to cook what I have left. After that my son and I will starve."

Elijah told her, "Don't worry. Go home and cook what you have for you and your son. But first make a small cake for me. Then God will fill up your jar of flour and your bottle of olive oil again. And He will keep them filled until He sends rain again." So the widow went home and did what Elijah told her. She made a small cake and brought it to Elijah. Then she cooked the rest for herself and her son. When she went back to the kitchen, she saw that her jar of flour and her bottle of olive oil had been filled up again! She invited Elijah to stay with her, and they never ran out of food.

The Bottomless Jar of Oil

2 Kings 4:1-7

Elisha was a prophet who took over Elijah's mission. One day a woman went to Elisha in tears. "My husband loved the Lord," she told him. "But he owed a man some money before he died. Now that man has come to take my two sons away as slaves to pay for my husband's debt."

Elisha said, "I'll do my best to help you. What do you have left in your house?" "All I have is a little bottle of oil," she said. Elisha told her, "Go quickly and ask your neighbors for all their empty jars. Then go home and fill the jars with the oil you have left. Set each jar aside, and keep filling." So the woman collected as many jars as she could.

Her sons helped her, and then they began to fill the jars with oil. The oil did not stop flowing. They filled jar after jar after jar. "Give me another," the woman told her sons. "But mother," they said, "we have used them all."

So the woman went back to Elisha. "What do I do now?" she asked him. "Go sell all your jars of olive oil. And you can give the man what you owe him. You and your sons can live on whatever is left."

ESTHER

- Mentioned in: The Book of Esther
- Meaning of name: Esther's birth name was Hadassah, which means "myrtle tree." Esther means "star."
- She lived in: Ancient Persia
- Related to: Mordecai, her cousin, who was her guardian for many years
- Married to: Xerxes, king of Persia

Milestones:

Esther saved her people from destruction by bravely facing the evil Haman.

Questions:

In the Book of Esther, God's actions and guiding hand are felt by Esther and Mordecai, although He is not mentioned directly. Do you feel God acting in your life even though you don't see Him? Do you know of someone who has risked his or her life for somebody else?

Then Queen Esther answered, "If I have found favor with you, Your Majesty, and if it pleases you, grant me my life—this is my petition. And spare my people—this is my request."
Esther 7:3

The Proud King

Esther 1:1-8

Xerxes was king of Persia. He ruled over many people, and he had a grand palace in the capital city of Susa. One day he decided to give a big celebration to show off all his wealth. He invited his officials and officers. The dinner was such a success that the king decided to make the festivities last one hundred and eighty days. After that, the king gave a seven-day banquet. He invited everyone from the city of Susa to come no matter who they were.

The king opened up his palace gardens and had tables laid out full of delicious food. The cups were made of gold, and each one had a different pattern. The garden was decorated with colorful blue and white curtains that swooped between the tall columns. The floors were made of marble and adorned in jewels. There were couches made of gold and silver. Everyone who came was very impressed. When the royal wine was brought out, the king said to the people, "Drink as much as you want!"

139

Queen Vashti Disobeys

Esther 1:10-21

By the seventh day, the king and his guests were in a good mood from all the wine. "Bring out my wife," the king said to his servants. "Let me show everyone how beautiful and rich she looks with the royal crown on her head."

The servants went to Queen Vashti and told her what her husband had said, but Queen Vashti didn't want to go. So she stayed in her rooms. The servants went back and told the king. He was angry that his wife had refused him in front of all his guests. "Your Majesty," the officials told the king, "her behavior is terrible.

She is insulting you and every other husband in the kingdom.
You should make a law against that kind of behavior. Vashti
should not be your queen anymore, and
you should pick someone else more
worthy than Vashti to be queen." The
king liked this idea and agreed to it.

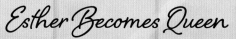

Esther Becomes Queen

Esther 2:1-17

King Xerxes began his search for a new queen. He had his officials round up the most beautiful young women in the kingdom. Esther was one of them. Esther was a Hebrew woman who had been raised by her cousin Mordecai after her parents died.

When Esther arrived at the palace, the king chose her along with his other favorites to stay with him for a whole year.

They were flooded with gifts of expensive perfumes and scented oils. They each had a room with their own maids, and every day they had a beauty treatment to make them even more beautiful.

During this time Mordecai walked by the courtyard everyday to make sure Esther was okay. Then he would remind her not to tell anyone, especially the king, that she was a Hebrew.

When it was Esther's turn to meet privately with the king, she was so charming and gracious that he fell in love with her. Her beauty outshone the others. "I have found my new bride," he told all his officials. Then he put the crown on her head and made Esther queen.

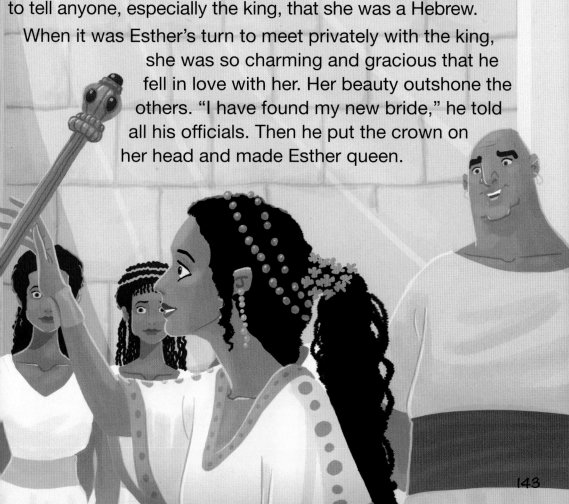

144

Haman's Order

Esther 2:19-3:15

After Esther had become queen, her cousin Mordecai was made a palace official. But the king gave the highest position in his palace to a man named Haman. Everyone was ordered to kneel down to Haman. But when Mordecai's turn came to kneel, he would not do it. "Why aren't you kneeling down like you were told?" the other officials asked him.

"Because I am a Hebrew," Mordecai said. "And I don't kneel to anyone but God." Haman was furious. He couldn't believe that someone had dishonored him. When he found out that it was because Mordecai was Jewish, he came up with a plan. Haman went to the king and said, "The Jews in your kingdom are different from everybody else. They won't follow the king's laws or obey the rules. We can't put up with it anymore; let's kill them all."

"You have my permission," replied the king. "Do whatever you want." So Haman sent out an announcement to everyone in the kingdom that read: All Jewish men and women and their children are to be killed on the thirteenth day of the first month.

Esther Has a Plan

Esther 4:1-5:4

Mordecai heard about Haman's order to kill the Jews. He tore up his clothes and went through Susa wailing and crying. When Esther heard about this, she sent a servant in the city square to ask him why he was so distraught. Mordecai said to Esther's servant, "Tell Esther that our people, the Jews, are going to be murdered and that she must beg the king to save them!"

When Esther received Mordecai's message, she immediately sent one back in return: "No one is allowed to see the king

without being invited. It could cost me my life if I go to the king uninvited!" But Mordecai replied, "You are a Jew, Esther, and if you don't speak now, you will be dead, too. Maybe you are queen right now so that you can save your people."

Esther decided to go to the king uninvited even if it meant she might die. Though Esther was afraid, the king was happily surprised to see his beautiful queen and said: "My darling, what brings you here? Whatever it is, I promise to give it to you."

"Come to dinner tonight," Esther answered, "and bring Haman with you."

Esther Saves Her People

Esther 7:1-6

Esther dined with the king and Haman.
They ate and drank together. And finally
as they were finishing their meal, the king
said, "Esther, what can I do for you? You
have pleased me so much that I would
give you half my kingdom if you asked."

Esther knew this was the moment.
"Your Majesty," she said. "If you love me, then
I ask you to do one thing for me. Save my people.
There is an order going around the kingdom that we
must die." "Who would dare order such a thing?"
the king asked. "Haman is the cruel-hearted one
who is out to get us!" Esther said.

Suddenly Haman looked terrified.

149

Haman Is Punished

Esther 7:7–8:2

The king was so angry that he stormed off to the gardens. Haman knew that it was no use to chase after him. He stayed and pleaded with Esther for his life. He dropped to his knees on the ground in front of her. But just then the king came back in the room. "Look at you," the king shouted. "Now you are even bullying my wife right here in my own palace!"

So the king gave an order for Haman to be hung on the tower Haman had built for Mordecai. The king gave Esther everything that once belonged to Haman. He also made Mordecai one of his highest officials. He took his signet that once was Haman's and put it on Mordecai's finger, and Esther appointed Mordecai to be in charge of Haman's property.

A Time to Celebrate

Esther 8:3-17; 9:1-28

King Xerxes said to Esther and Mordecai, "Now you can't change a law that is sealed with my ring. But you can make another law so that the Jews can defend themselves. You have the signet ring. Save your people!"

So Mordecai made a new law to protect the Jews. Secretaries wrote the new law down and messengers rode out as fast as they could, spreading the announcement. All the Jewish people of the kingdom had big parties and celebrated when they got the news. They united together, and other people became afraid of the Jews, and God kept them safe.

The New Testament

A Baby for Elizabeth

Luke 1:5-25

The priest Zechariah and his wife, Elizabeth, lived in Judea. They loved the Lord, but they had no children, and they were both growing old.

One day when Zechariah was chosen to go into the temple of the Lord and burn incense, he saw an angel standing by the altar. He was terrified, but the angel said, "Don't be afraid, Zechariah! Your wife is going to have a son, and you are to name him John. He will be a special person. God is going to use him to help people see the truth and to prepare the way for the Lord." Zechariah didn't know what to think. "How can this be true? My wife and I are too old to have children," he said to the angel.

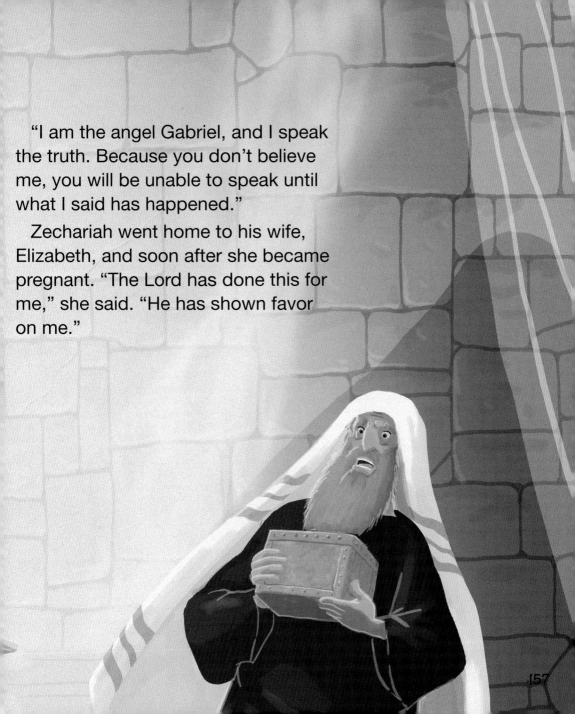

"I am the angel Gabriel, and I speak the truth. Because you don't believe me, you will be unable to speak until what I said has happened."

Zechariah went home to his wife, Elizabeth, and soon after she became pregnant. "The Lord has done this for me," she said. "He has shown favor on me."

MARY
THE MOTHER OF JESUS

- Mentioned in: Matthew, Mark, Luke, and John
- Meaning of name: The same meaning as the name *Miriam* (see page 62)
- She lived in: Nazareth in ancient Israel
- Married to: Joseph

Milestones:

Mary was visited by an angel. She was chosen by God to give birth to Jesus, who would go on to redeem mankind through dying on the cross. She was humble and courageous to risk being an unwed mother at that time. She could have been stoned to death. She had courage and strength, watching Jesus grow up, observing His ministry, and eventually seeing Him die and rise from the dead and ascend to heaven.

Questions:

Do you think Mary felt troubled by knowing that Jesus had to die on the cross? Do you think that she had to be courageous to be the mother of Jesus?

While they were there, the time came for the baby to be born, and she gave birth to her firstborn, a son. She wrapped him in cloths and placed him in a manger, because there was no guest room available for them.
Luke 2:6-7

An Angel Visits Mary

Luke 1:26-38

The angel Gabriel went to the town of Nazareth. He had a message for a young woman named Mary. "Greetings," he told her. "You are truly blessed!" But Mary was frightened. She had never seen an angel before and didn't know what he was talking about. "Don't be afraid. The Lord is with you," the angel said. "He has sent me to tell you that you will give birth to a son. He will be called the Son of God. And God will make Him a king just like His ancestor David. But His kingdom will never end."

"How can I have a child?" Mary asked him. "I haven't been with a man."

The angel answered, "The Holy Spirit will make it happen. That's why the child will be called the Son of God. Nothing is impossible for God! Even your relative Elizabeth, who is barren, is going to have a child in her old age."

"I am God's servant," Mary said. "I will do whatever He wants." Then the angel, Gabriel, left her.

ELIZABETH

- Mentioned in: Luke
- Meaning of name: God's promise
- She lived in: Judea, Israel
- Related to: Mary the mother of Jesus
- Married to: Zachariah the priest
- Mother of: John the Baptist

Milestones:

Elizabeth gave birth to John the Baptist in her old age. She had to endure nine months of her husband's silence while he was unable to speak.

Have you ever been overwhelmed by some news and needed someone to confide in? Was there someone there for you like the kindly Elizabeth? Have you been there for someone else?

When Elizabeth heard Mary's greeting, the baby leaped in her womb, and Elizabeth was filled with the Holy Spirit. In a loud voice she exclaimed: "Blessed are you among women, and blessed is the child you will bear!"
Luke 1:41-42

Mary and Elizabeth

Luke 1:39-56

Mary soon traveled to Judea to find her relative Elizabeth. "I have heard the news! The Lord is blessing you with a baby," Mary told her. When Elizabeth heard Mary's voice, the baby leaped in her belly, and Elizabeth was filled with the Holy Spirit. She exclaimed loudly, "Mary, you are blessed among women, and so is your child! You believed that the Lord would fulfill His promises! Why am I so favored that the mother of my Lord should come to me?" Mary stayed with Elizabeth and Zachariah for three months. Then she went back to Nazareth and was married to Joseph.

Jesus Is Born

Luke 2:1-7

The Emperor of Rome had ordered that everyone must list their families in the record books. People had to register in their hometowns. So Joseph left Nazareth and went to Bethlehem, the hometown of his ancestor King David. Mary came with him. It was almost time for her to give birth.

After they arrived, Mary gave birth to Jesus in the place where animals were kept because there was no room anywhere else. She wrapped Him in cloths so He wouldn't be cold. Then she placed Him in a feeding trough.

The Shepherds

Luke 2:8-20

That night a few shepherds were out in the fields with their sheep. Suddenly the angel of the Lord came and showered them with light. They were frightened and hid their faces. "Don't be afraid," the angel said. "I have brought good news. Today in King David's town, a baby has been born. He is Christ the Lord. Go and worship Him. You'll find Him asleep on a bed of hay." Then the angel of the Lord was joined by other angels all singing praises to God. "Praise God in heaven," they sang. "He gives His peace to people on earth who will receive it." Then they left and went back to God. The shepherds were left alone in the dark night. But the light still twinkled in their eyes. "Let's go and see what the angel was talking about," they said to each other.

They went to Bethlehem and found Jesus asleep on the hay. "The angel said, 'He is Christ the Lord,'" the shepherds told Mary. Then they bowed down and worshiped the child. Mary listened to the shepherds and stored up their words like treasures in her heart. Then the shepherds left, but the whole way home they kept praising the Lord.

The Wise Men

Matthew 2:1-12

After Jesus was born, wise men arrived in Jerusalem in search of Jesus. They went to Herod's palace and asked, "Where is the newborn king of the Jews? We have seen His star in the East, and we have come to worship Him." King Herod was terrified! A new king? He asked his advisors where the Christ would be born. "In Bethlehem," they said. So King Herod told the wise men, "Go to Bethlehem. Search for the child, and when you find Him, come back and tell me. I want to go and worship Him too."

The wise men left for Bethlehem, following the bright star until it stopped over the place where Jesus lived with Mary and Joseph.

When the wise men saw baby Jesus, they knelt down to worship Him, and they laid their gifts at His feet. They had brought gold, frankincense, and myrrh from their country in the East.

That night while the wise men were asleep, an angel warned them in a dream not to go back to King Herod. So the wise men returned home by a different road.

Jesus of Nazareth

Matthew 2:13-23; Luke 2:40

King Herod waited for the wise men to come back and tell him where Jesus lived. But they never came. He thought they had tricked him, and he became furious. He did not want Jesus to grow up and become a rival king to him. So he ordered his soldiers to kill all baby boys in Bethlehem. That night an angel came to Joseph in a dream. "Get up!" the angel said. "Take the child and his mother and flee to Egypt. King Herod is looking for Jesus. He wants to kill Him!" Joseph immediately jumped out of bed and woke up Mary. They loaded their donkey with the few things they owned and left for Egypt.

Sometime later an angel came to Joseph again in a dream. "It's safe to return to Israel," the angel told him. "King Herod has died, and there is no more danger." The angel told Joseph not to return to Bethlehem. So Joseph and Mary went back to Nazareth and raised Jesus in that town, and He grew up healthy and happy.

Jesus in the Temple

Luke 2:41-52

Mary and Joseph went to Jerusalem every year for Passover. When Jesus was twelve, He came with them. After the celebration was over, Mary and Joseph got ready to go back to Nazareth. They thought Jesus was with some of their friends who were traveling back too. But their friends said, "No, we haven't seen Him." So Mary started to panic. "Oh no, we've lost Him," she cried. They began to search all over Jerusalem.

Three days later they found Jesus in the temple. He was talking with the teachers and asking them questions. Everyone in the temple was amazed by His wisdom.

"Son," Mary cried out when she saw Him, "why did You scare us like this? We've been looking for You everywhere!"

Jesus replied, "Why did you have to look? Didn't you know that I would be in My Father's house?" Then He went with His parents back to Nazareth, and Mary kept thinking about what Jesus had said.

John the Baptist
Luke 1:5-25; John 1:19-28

Before Mary was told she would be expecting Jesus, the angel Gabriel also visited a priest named Zechariah in the temple in Jerusalem. The angel promised him and his wife, Elizabeth, a son. Elizabeth was a relative of Mary, and she

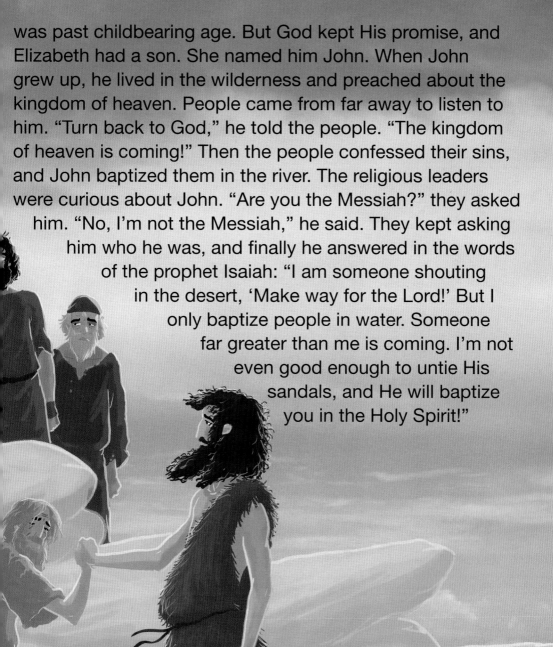

was past childbearing age. But God kept His promise, and Elizabeth had a son. She named him John. When John grew up, he lived in the wilderness and preached about the kingdom of heaven. People came from far away to listen to him. "Turn back to God," he told the people. "The kingdom of heaven is coming!" Then the people confessed their sins, and John baptized them in the river. The religious leaders were curious about John. "Are you the Messiah?" they asked him. "No, I'm not the Messiah," he said. They kept asking him who he was, and finally he answered in the words of the prophet Isaiah: "I am someone shouting in the desert, 'Make way for the Lord!' But I only baptize people in water. Someone far greater than me is coming. I'm not even good enough to untie His sandals, and He will baptize you in the Holy Spirit!"

Jesus Is Baptized

Matthew 3:13-16; John 1:29-35

One day Jesus came to be baptized too. But John refused, saying, "Jesus, you should be the one baptizing me!"

"It is right for us to do this. It carries out God's holy plan," Jesus answered. So John baptized Jesus in the Jordan River. As Jesus lifted his head from the water, the sky opened up. Then the Spirit of God came down from heaven like a dove, and the voice of God said, "This is My beloved Son, and I am pleased with Him."

The next day John saw Jesus coming toward him. John turned to the people and said, "This is the man I told you about when I said, 'He is greater than I am.' He is the Lamb of God, the one who takes away your sins."

Then John said, "I didn't realize He was the one until yesterday. God, who sent me to baptize with water, told me, 'The one on whom you see the Spirit descend upon and rest is the one who will baptize with the Holy Spirit.'"

Jesus Turns Water into Wine

John 2:1-11

Jesus went to a wedding in Galilee with His disciples. His mother Mary was also there. In the evening, the wine ran out, so Mary went to Jesus and said, "There's no more wine." "My time has not come yet." He answered. But Mary told the servants, "Do whatever Jesus tells you!"

There were six big, empty jars in the house. Jesus told the servants to fill them up with water. When that was done, He said, "Give a drink to the man who is in charge of the feast." The servants obeyed.

As the man took a sip from the cup, he called to the groom and said, "What a surprise! Most people offer the best wine first and the cheap wine last. But you have saved the best for last."

This was the first of many miracles Jesus would perform to reveal His glory, and the disciples believed in Him.

The Water of Life

John 4:4-26

Jesus was traveling with His disciples through Samaria. They came upon the same field that Jacob had given his son Joseph long ago. Jacob's well was still there. Jesus sat down for a rest while His disciples went out to find food. Just then a Samaritan woman came to fetch water from the well. "Would you give Me a drink?" Jesus asked her.

"But You are a Jew," she answered, "and I am a Samaritan. How can You ask me to give You water?" Jews and Samaritans did not associate with each other. Jesus told her, "If you knew who I was, then you might be the one asking Me for a drink. I give the water of life to those who thirst." "Sir," the woman said, "if You give life-giving water, then where's the bucket You use to fetch it with?" Jesus answered, "My water is not from a well. Whoever drinks water from that well will only get thirsty again. The water I give is eternal life. You'll never need another drink again." But the woman just shrugged. "When the one they call Christ comes, He can explain all these things to us," she said.

"Here I am," Jesus told her. "I am speaking to you now."

183

Jesus Heals a Crippled Man
Luke 5:17-26

One day Jesus was teaching a group of people who had come from all over Israel to meet Him. The crowd gathered into one room, and soon there was no place left to stand or sit. Four men came carrying their paralyzed friend on a mat. But there were too many people, so the crippled man did not get to see Jesus. Then his friends had an idea. They removed some tiles on the roof and lowered the man down through the ceiling.

When Jesus saw how much faith they had, He said to the crippled man, "Friend, your sins are forgiven." The Pharisees

heard that and became angry. "Who does He think He is?" they said to each other. "Only God can forgive sins." Jesus looked at them and said, "Why do you say such things? What is easiest? To forgive his sins or tell him to start walking? But so that you will know that the Son of Man has been given authority to forgive sins, I say: Pick up your mat and walk home!" The man started to stand up. His crippled legs had been healed, and he could walk!

People were amazed, and they praised God saying, "We have seen a miracle today!"

Planting Seeds

Mark 4:1-20

While Jesus was teaching by the Sea of Galilee, He told them this story: "A farmer went out to scatter his seeds. Some seeds fell on the road, but the birds came and ate them up. Some seeds fell between the rocks. They sprouted but died quickly because there was not enough deep soil to grow strong roots. Some seeds fell among the thorn bushes and were choked as they started to grow. But some of the farmer's seeds fell on good ground. These seeds turned into a great harvest, 30 to 100 times more than what had been planted."

The disciples didn't understand the meaning of Jesus' story, so He later explained it to them. "Some people are like the seeds on the road. They hear My words, but then the devil comes and takes it away from them. Some are like the seeds falling between the rocks; they believe, but when they suffer hardships because of their faith, they fall away.

The seeds being choked by the thorn bushes are like people who believe, but let worries and desires for wealth and riches choke their faith. But others are like the seeds sown on good ground. They hear My word and live by it. And they make My Father happy."

True Happiness

Matthew 5:1-12

Jesus went up to the side of the mountain where all the people had gathered to hear Him speak.

"My friends," Jesus said, "God blesses those who look to Him for help. They belong to the kingdom of heaven! God blesses those who feel sad and hopeless. He will comfort them! God blesses those who are humble. They belong to God!

God blesses those who obey Him. They will be given what they ask for! God blesses those who are forgiving and show mercy to others. They will be treated with forgiveness and mercy! God blesses those whose hearts are pure. They will see Him! God blesses those who make peace. They will be called His children! God blesses those who are treated badly for doing what is right. They too belong to God's kingdom! Be happy! Feel excited and joyful today! For those who do what is right by God will have a big reward in the kingdom of heaven."

Being Salt and Light

Matthew 5:13-16

Jesus said to His friends, "You are the salt of the earth. What would salt be like if it didn't taste salty? You might as well throw it out and walk over it. You too will be useless unless you do as you should. Forgive the people that do you wrong. Love each other. Share what you have with others."

After a pause Jesus continued, "You are the shining light that illuminates the world. No one would light a lamp and put it under a clay pot, would they? All the light would be hidden, and no one would be able to see. A lamp is placed on a lamp stand where it can give light to everything in the house. Let your light shine bright. Share your light with others. They will see the good you do, and they will give praise to your Father in heaven."

Do Not Worry

Matthew 6:19-30

Jesus was speaking to a large crowd that had gathered outside one morning.

He said, "All the things you have here on earth are of little worth. A moth can come and chew your clothes. Rust can ruin your favorite things, and thieves can come and steal your money. Don't store up these things that can be taken from you. Treasures in heaven cannot be destroyed or taken from you. Give your heart to God alone! You cannot love riches and God at the same time. Have faith that God will take care of you. He will give you everything you need."

"Look at the birds in the sky. Aren't they cheerful and happy? They don't work all the time, and yet God takes care of them! Look at the wildflowers. They don't worry about

clothes, yet even Solomon didn't look as fine and colorful as they do! God takes care of everything that grows, even if it only lives for a day. If He does that for the birds and the flowers, He will certainly take care of you too."

The House on the Rock

Matthew 7:24-29

Jesus said, "Anyone who hears and obeys these teachings of Mine is like the wise man who built his house on solid rock. Rain poured down, rivers rose up, and winds beat against that house. Why did it stay standing?

Because it was built on firm ground! Obey My
teachings, and they will be like a solid rock for you."
Anyone who hears My teachings and still disobeys will
be like the foolish man who built his house on sand. Rain
poured down, rivers rose up, and winds beat against that
house, and it crumbled right to the ground. The foolish man
does not remain strong in his faith in God when he comes
upon problems."

God's Kingdom Is Like a Seed

Mark 4:26-32

Jesus said, "This is what the kingdom of God is like. A farmer plants seeds in his field. Even while the farmer is asleep," Jesus said, "the seeds he scattered keep growing from the soil that nurtures them. Take a look at a mustard seed! It's a very small seed. But when it is fully grown, it is huge. Even the birds build nests in its big leafy branches!"

The Storm

Mark 4:35-38

Jesus was with His disciples
on Lake Galilee. The sky was
growing dark, and Jesus said, "Let's cross
to the other side." While they were crossing, a
storm started to blow. Waves splashed and filled the
inside of the boat with water. The boat got heavier and
heavier and was about to sink.

"Jesus, help us!" the disciples cried. But Jesus was
asleep at the back of the boat. He didn't hear them.
The storm was growing worse, so they woke Him up.
"Teacher," they said, "don't You care that we drown?"

Jesus Calms the Storm

Mark 4:39-41

When Jesus woke up, He didn't panic like the disciples. He stood up and held out His hands.

Then He told the waves, "Be quiet!" And He told the wind, "Be still!" All at once the sea stopped thrashing, and the wind stopped howling. It was calm and peaceful again.

Jesus turned back around to His disciples and said, "Why were you afraid? Don't you have faith?"

The disciples were terrified and asked each other, "Who is this man? Even the wind and the waves obey Him!"

A Sick Woman

Mark 5:21-34

Jesus went to teach by the shore of Lake Galilee. A man named Jairus, who had a sick daughter, came to see Jesus. "Please come to my home," he said to Jesus. "My daughter could die any minute. Please come and place Your hands on her so she will be healed and live." Jesus agreed to help.

On the way to Jairus' home, a sickly woman tried to get Jesus' attention. There were far too many people though. No doctor could heal her, and she believed if only she touched Jesus then she would be healed. So she touched His robe, and instantly the sickness left her body.

"Who touched Me?" Jesus said. The woman knelt down before Him in fear, telling Him that it was her. "Dear woman," Jesus said, "your faith has healed you. Go in peace and be free from your suffering."

A Dying Girl

Mark 5:35-43

Finally Jesus reached Jairus' home. Some men came out of the house and told Jairus, "It's too late. Your daughter is dead."

But Jesus didn't listen to them. He told Jairus, "Don't worry. Just have faith!" Then He went inside the house. The little girl's family was sitting around crying. "Why are you so sad?" Jesus asked them. "The girl is only asleep."

Jesus went into the girl's bedroom. He picked up her hand and said, "Talitha, koum!" which means, "Little girl, get up!" Suddenly the little girl opened her eyes and sat up. She got out of bed and started walking around. Her parents were amazed. Jesus told them to give the little girl something to eat. "But keep this miracle that you have seen to yourself," Jesus added. "Don't tell anyone." Then He left.

206

Jesus Seeks a Quiet Place

Mark 6:30-33

The disciples were sitting with Jesus. They were telling Him about their day and all the things they had done and taught. People were walking by with noisy carts and animals. So Jesus said, "Let's go find a quiet place where we can be alone and get some rest."

They left town and went down to the lake. Then they got in their boat to look for a quiet place. But the people from town saw them leave. They said to each other, "Come on. Let's follow Jesus!" People from other villages left what they were doing and came too. A few of them had an idea of where Jesus and the disciples were going. So the whole crowd ran ahead and got there first. There were five thousand of them.

The Hungry People

Mark 6:34-38; John 6:5-9

When the disciples saw the big crowd, they groaned. But Jesus didn't mind. He felt compassion for them. They were like sheep without a shepherd. So He told them to come closer, and then He began to teach. Afternoon rolled around, and the disciples were hungry. "Let's take a break," they

told Jesus. "The people can go back to their villages and eat something." But Jesus said, "Why don't you give them something to eat?" "That's impossible," they replied. "It would cost a fortune to feed all these people!" The disciple Andrew said, "Well, there is a boy here with some food. He has five loaves of bread and two fish. But that's not enough to feed five thousand people."

Five Loaves and Two Fish

Mark 6:39-44; John 6:10-14

Jesus told His disciples to have faith. "Tell the people to find a nice spot in the grass and sit down," He said. So the disciples obeyed. Once the people quieted down, Jesus stood up, took a loaf of bread in His hands, and gave thanks to God. Then He broke the bread and gave it to the

disciples, who passed it around to the people. He continued until every single person had a piece. Then He did the same with the fish.

There was plenty of food, and the people couldn't eat it all. Jesus told His disciples to not let anything go to waste. So they went around and gathered up the extra food in big baskets. The people were amazed when they saw Jesus' miracle. "How did He make so much food out of so little?" they wondered. "It was a miracle! He must be the Prophet whom God has promised to send to the world!"

Jesus Walks on Water

Mark 6:45-50

When the day was done, Jesus told His disciples to go home without Him. He wanted to be by Himself for a while. They said goodbye and got in their boat. When all the crowds had left, Jesus climbed up to the side of the mountain and prayed.

That evening Jesus was still by Himself on the mountainside. He could see the lake from where He sat, and

He spotted His disciples in their boat. The wind was very strong, and they were having trouble rowing. So Jesus went down to help them. He started to walk on top of the water toward them. But when the disciples saw Him, they were scared. "It's a ghost!" they cried out. They clung to each other's arm and trembled. "It's me!" Jesus told them. "Don't be afraid."

A Second Chance

John 8:1-11

Early one morning Jesus went to the temple where He usually went to teach. People were crowding around to hear Him. Suddenly a group of angry men burst through the gate. They were holding a woman roughly by the arm. "Teacher!" they shouted. "This woman has been caught with a man who was not her husband. This woman should be stoned for her sins! What do You say?" They asked Jesus this question because they wanted to test Him. Would He say yes or no?

But Jesus said neither. Instead He looked around at the crowd that had gathered and said, "Let the person who has

never sinned throw the first stone!" Then He bent down and wrote something with His finger in the sand. The men were speechless. They looked around at one another, but no one volunteered to throw the first stone because they all had sinned. One by one the men walked away until only Jesus and the woman were left. "Isn't there anyone left to accuse you?" Jesus asked the woman. The woman shook her head. "I will not accuse you either," Jesus said. "You are forgiven, but go and sin no more!"

A Woman Washes Jesus' Feet

Luke 7:36-40

A Pharisee named Simon invited Jesus to have dinner with him. There was a woman who had heard that Jesus was at Simon's house. She was a sinful woman, and everyone in the village looked down on her. She went to Simon's house and brought an expensive bottle of perfume. When the woman saw Jesus, she kneeled down on the floor near His feet and began to cry. Her tears fell on Jesus' feet, and she washed them with her tears and dried them with her hair.

Next the woman poured her expensive perfume on Jesus' feet, and she covered them with her kisses.

Simon had been watching all of this. "If Jesus were really a prophet of God," Simon thought, "He would know what kind of a sinner this woman was." Jesus knew what Simon was thinking. He said, "Simon, I'd like to tell you a story."

Love and Forgiveness

Luke 7:41-50

Jesus began to tell a story to Simon the Pharisee. "Two people owed money to a moneylender," Jesus said. "One of them owed five hundred silver coins, and the other owed fifty, but neither of them had the money to pay him back. The moneylender decided that since they didn't have the money, he would forgive their debts. Which one of the men was more grateful to the moneylender?" Jesus asked Simon. "The man that owed five hundred silver coins," Simon answered, "because he owed so much more."

Jesus smiled and said, "Now Simon, have you noticed this woman? From the moment I arrived she has been with Me, washing and kissing My feet. She has even poured expensive perfume on them! You did not do any of these things. She is like the one who owed five hundred silver coins and did not have to pay any of them back. That is why she shows great love!" Then Jesus turned to the woman and said, "Your sins are forgiven. Because of your faith, you are saved."

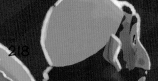

Let the Children Come to Me

Mark 10:13-16

Many parents brought their children to Jesus hoping He would bless them. The children crowded around Jesus, but Jesus' disciples told them to stop. "Step back," they instructed the children. Jesus doesn't want to be bothered."

But Jesus said, "Let the children come to Me! Don't stop them. These children belong to the kingdom of God. None of you can enter God's kingdom unless you accept it the way a child does. Learn from them!"

Then Jesus opened His arms and the little children ran giggling and smiling, wrapping their arms around Jesus' neck. Jesus placed His hands on them and blessed each one.

Following Jesus
Mark 10:23-31

Jesus said to His disciples, "It is easier for a camel to go through the eye of a needle than it is for a rich person to get into God's kingdom." The disciples were amazed. "But how can anyone ever be saved?" they cried. Jesus replied, "With people, this is impossible. But not with God. All things are possible with God."

Peter said, "We left everything to follow you, Jesus!"

"Anyone who gives up his home or his family or the things he owns for Me will be rewarded. You may be mistreated and persecuted because of Me, but in the world to come you will receive one hundred times as much as you gave up for Me! Many who are last here on earth will be first in heaven. And many who are first now will later be last."

The Good Shepherd

John 10:11-18

Jesus said, "I am the good shepherd, and you are My flock. The shepherd will give up His life for His sheep. But hired workers don't own the sheep, so they do not care about them. When a wolf comes, they run off and leave the sheep to be taken and eaten. But each little sheep is important to Me.

If one is lost, I will search high and low until that sheep is found! I love My sheep, and they love Me just as the Father loves Me, and I love the Father. I bring all My sheep together into one flock and watch over them. I will gladly give up My life for My sheep. No one takes My life from Me. I give it up willingly! I have the power to give up My life and the power to receive it back again just as My Father commanded Me to do."

MARY & MARTHA

- Mentioned in: Luke and John
- Meaning of name: Mary carries the same meaning as Miriam, while Martha means "lady" or "mistress."
- They lived in: Bethany in ancient Israel
- Related to: Lazarus, whom Jesus raised from the dead

Milestones:

Mary sat at Jesus' feet and listened to His teachings, while Martha invited Him into her home and prepared food for Him. They were some of Jesus' closest friends.

Jesus said that Mary was right to sit down and listen to His teachings, even when Martha wanted her to help prepare food. What do you think it was like to sit at the feet of Jesus to listen to Him? Do you find it easier to be busy with many things than to be quiet and listen to God?

"Martha, Martha," the Lord answered, "you are worried and upset about many things, but few things are needed—or indeed only one. Mary has chosen what is better, and it will not be taken away from her."
Luke 10:41-42

Mary and Martha

Luke 10:38-42

Jesus and His disciples had traveled for a long time and were tired. When they came to the village of Bethany, they stopped to rest.

Martha and Mary were two sisters who lived in Bethany. They welcomed Jesus and His disciples to stay in their home. Martha rushed around, dusting and sweeping and cooking and cleaning.

Martha's sister, Mary, was so excited to see Jesus that she sat right down on the floor in front of Him. As Jesus spoke, Mary listened to every word He said. Martha was annoyed by this. "Jesus, don't you care that Mary is doing nothing and leaving me to do all the work?" Martha said. "Tell her to help me."

Jesus answered, "Martha, you are worried about all of these things you are doing, but only one thing is necessary. Mary has chosen what is best, and I will not make her stop."

The Death of Lazarus

John 11:1-16

Mary and Martha had a brother named Lazarus. He was one of Jesus' good friends. But one day Lazarus got very sick. So Mary and Martha sent a message and told Jesus to come. Jesus got the news, but although he loved Mary and Martha and Lazarus, He didn't go right away. He knew that Lazarus would be alright.

Two days later Jesus told His disciples to come with Him to see Lazarus. "But he lives in Judea," they answered. "Why do You want to go? Only a few days ago the Jewish leaders in Judea were trying to kill You."

Jesus answered, "Our friend Lazarus is asleep. I want to wake him up."

"If he sleeps he'll get better, won't he?" His disciples asked. But they didn't understand what Jesus meant. "No, Lazarus is dead," He explained. "But I'm glad I wasn't there when he died, because now you will have a good reason to put your faith in Me. Let's go, and I'll show you."

Jesus Brings Lazarus to Life

John 11:17-44

When Martha saw that Jesus was coming, she ran out to meet Him. Jesus said, "I am the one who can raise the dead! Anyone who puts their faith in Me will live, even after death. Do you believe this, Martha?" "Yes, Lord!" she replied. "I know that You are the Son of God."

Then Mary came out. She went to Jesus and kneeled down in front of Him. "Lord, our brother is dead. If You had come sooner, I know he would've lived." Jesus was moved and started to weep. Then He walked over to Lazarus' tomb.

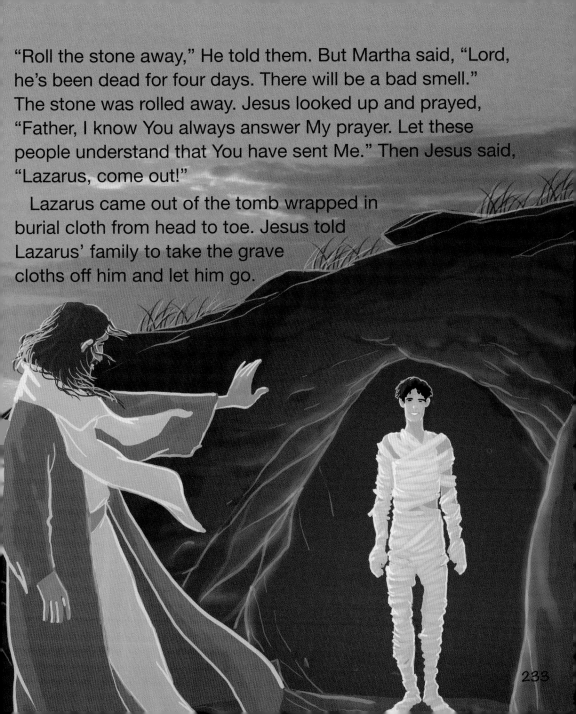

"Roll the stone away," He told them. But Martha said, "Lord, he's been dead for four days. There will be a bad smell." The stone was rolled away. Jesus looked up and prayed, "Father, I know You always answer My prayer. Let these people understand that You have sent Me." Then Jesus said, "Lazarus, come out!"

Lazarus came out of the tomb wrapped in burial cloth from head to toe. Jesus told Lazarus' family to take the grave cloths off him and let him go.

Who Gave the Most?

Mark 12:41-44

Jesus was in the temple near the offering box. He was watching people put in their money gifts to God. The rich people put in handfuls of money. The coins clinked and

clanked as they fell into the box. Then a poor widow went up to the box. She put in the only two coins she had, which were worth about two pennies.

Jesus told His disciples to gather around. Then He said, "This poor widow has put in more than all the others." The disciples shook their heads and said, "She only put in two small coins!"

Jesus nodded. Then He said, "You see, the many coins of the rich do not mean much. They are like loose change in their pockets. But the few coins of the poor are as valuable as gold. And this widow gave away everything she had to live on."

The Good Samaritan

Luke 10:29-37

One day an expert of the law wanted to test Jesus. "What must I do to get eternal life?" he asked Jesus. "You shall love the Lord your God with all your heart, and your soul, and your mind," answered Jesus, "And you shall love your neighbor as yourself." "Who is my neighbor?" said the teacher to justify himself. Jesus looked at him and said, "A man was traveling along a deserted road. Robbers came by and attacked him. They stole everything he had and left him lying in a pitiful heap by the roadside. Then they ran off. A priest was traveling down the road and came upon the man. He crossed over to the other side and kept on walking. Next, a temple worker came upon the man. He also crossed to the other side of the road and kept on walking. Finally, a Samaritan came by. When he saw the man, he stopped to help him. He treated his wounds with oil and wine and took him to an inn. He told the innkeeper, 'Please care for the man, and I will pay you however much it costs.'"

"Now," Jesus continued, "which of these three men would you say acted as a neighbor?"

The man who had asked the question said, "The one who showed pity."

Jesus answered, "Yes! Now go and do the same."

237

A Rich Fool

Luke 12:13-21

A young man in the crowd stood up and called to Jesus, "Teacher, tell my brother to be fair and give my share of what our father has left us!"

Jesus answered, "If I did that, it would not help you. What you own will not make your life any better than it is. Then Jesus continued, "There was a farmer who produced a harvest so big that he had to build several new barns just

to hold the grain. But God said to him, 'You fool! This night you'll die. What good is all your wealth then?' This is how it will be with anyone who stores up riches for himself but is not rich in God."

Then Jesus said to the disciples, "Don't worry about your life, what you need to eat, drink, or wear—for your father in heaven will take care of you and give you everything you need."

Jesus Heals a Woman on the Sabbath

Luke 13:10-17

One Sabbath day, Jesus was teaching in a synagogue. A woman was there whose back was bent. She could hardly see Jesus because she was hunched over. "Come over here," Jesus told the woman. He put His hands on her, and the woman's back straightened. "You're well now!" Jesus said. The woman thanked God. But the synagogue leader was angry. He said to Jesus, "You can't heal someone on a Sabbath. There are six other days in which You can work, and people can come and be healed on those days. Why do You have to do it today?"

So Jesus said, "You all work on the Sabbath.

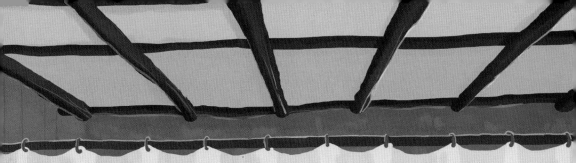

You untie your donkey and lead it to water no matter what day it is! This woman belongs to God. But Satan had bound her for eighteen years. Should she not be freed from her sickness because it is Sabbath?"

The synagogue leader and his friends were humiliated at Jesus' words. But the people in the crowd were delighted at the wonderful things Jesus was doing.

The Lost Sheep and the Lost Coin

Luke 15:1-10

One day when many tax collectors and other outcasts came to listen to Jesus, the Pharisees and the teachers of the Law started grumbling, "This man welcomes sinners and even eats with them!"

When Jesus heard them say these things, He turned and faced them.

"Imagine," Jesus said, "that you are a shepherd, and you have lost one of your sheep. Won't you leave the ninety-nine others behind and find the lost one? When you find the sheep, you will be so glad that you will carry it home on your shoulders. Then you will say to your friends, 'Let's celebrate! I've found the one that was lost.'" Jesus continued and said, "There is more rejoicing in heaven over one sinner that turns to God than over ninety-nine good people who do not need to. And what about a woman who loses one of her ten silver coins? Won't she light a lamp, sweep the floor, and look carefully until she has found it? My Father in heaven will celebrate when one of these sinners who sit with Me turns to Him."

The Loving Father

Luke 15:11-19

Jesus told another story:

A man had two sons. He loved them both and wanted to see them do well. He planned to divide his property and money between them. The younger son said, "Father, please give me my share. I want to go out in the world and become successful." He took off and traveled to a faraway country. He spent all his money on silly things. Before he knew it, he reached into his pocket, and there was no money left. Desperate for money, the younger son got a job working for a pig farmer. His clothes turned ragged and dirty. His stomach was always growling with hunger. He would've been happy to eat the slop from the trough of the pigs. At last he came to his senses. He thought, "This is foolish! My father treats his servants better than this! I will go to him and ask his forgiveness. Perhaps he will accept me, and I will offer to work for him."

So the son started on the long journey home again back to his father's house.

Forgiven

Luke 15:20-24, 25-32

Jesus continued telling the story:

The father spotted his youngest son walking toward home. He ran out to meet him and showered him in hugs and kisses. He called to his servants, "Bring out our finest clothes! Prepare a big feast! Put a shiny ring on my son's finger! He was lost, and now he is found!"

The older son was out in the field working. He ran back to the house to see what had happened. "What's going on?" he asked a servant. "Your brother is back!" the servants replied. The older brother became angry. He ran to his father and said, "I have been working like a slave for you. I have obeyed you. I have always done everything you asked me to. But my brother runs away, spends all your money and disobeys you. Why are you treating him like a prince?" His father answered, "Son, all I have is yours. You always did right and obeyed me. You were never lost, but your brother was lost. Be happy and celebrate with me. He has come back to us!"

Wheat and Weeds

Matthew 13:24-30, 36-39

Here is another story Jesus told: "Once, a farmer planted seeds in a field to grow wheat. After he left, an enemy came and planted weeds in that same field. The plants began to grow, and the weeds grew right along with the wheat. The servants of the farmer ran to him and said, 'Sir, why are there weeds growing among your grain?' The farmer replied, 'An enemy must have done this. Leave the weeds alone until harvest time. Otherwise you may pull up the wheat when you are trying to pull out the weeds. When the time is right, we will separate the two. We will burn the weeds and place the wheat in my barn.'"

Jesus explained, "The farmer's good seeds are like the people who hear My message and take it to heart. But the weeds are like the people who do not listen. Someday God will bring judgment to His people. God will separate them just like the farmer separated the weeds from his wheat."

A Woman's Faith

Matthew 15:21-28

Jesus was traveling with His disciples in the country of the Canaanites. A Canaanite woman walked behind them crying, "Lord, please have pity on me! I have a daughter, but she is full of evil spirits. Can You save her?" Jesus didn't say a word. The disciples told Jesus to send her away, but He said to her, "I have come to help the Israelites. They are like lost sheep. But you are a Canaanite." "Please help me," she said again.

"Would it be right to take away food from the children and give it to the dogs?" Jesus asked her. The woman replied, "No, Lord. But even dogs get the crumbs that fall from their owner's table."

Jesus knew that she truly trusted Him. "Dear woman," He said, "you have great faith! Go home—I've already given you what you've asked for."

God Shows Mercy

Luke 18:9-14

One day, Jesus told this story to some people who were overconfident in their own good behavior and righteousness. "Two men went into the temple to pray. One was a Pharisee, and the other was a tax collector. The Pharisee prayed, 'Thank you, God, for making me good. I am not greedy or dishonest. I am faithful in marriage, and I have always given part of my money to you.' But the tax collector stayed in the far corner of the temple. He did not think he was good enough to even look up toward heaven. He hung his head and prayed, 'God, have mercy on me! I am such a sinner.'

"I tell you," Jesus said. "The humble man, rather than the proud man, was forgiven by God. Those who are proud will be humbled by God, and those who are humble will be blessed by God."

A Job Well Done

Luke 19:15-26

Jesus told this parable: "A man of noble birth was going on a journey to a distant country to be made king. But first he summoned his three servants and gave them each the same amount of money. 'Put this money to work while I am away,' he said. And then he left. Later, after he was made king, he returned home and summoned his servants again. 'Tell me what you have done with the money I gave you.' The first servant made ten times the amount and was put in charge of ten cities. The second servant made five times the amount and was put in charge of five cities. The last servant made no money. 'I was afraid of you, so I didn't want to risk losing your money.' The king was angry. 'You could at least have put it in the bank,' he said. Then he ordered the money to be given to the first servant. 'But he already has plenty!' cried the king's officials.

The king replied, 'Those who do what I say will be given more. Those who are fearful and do nothing will lose what they had been given.'"

The Greatest in Heaven

Matthew 18:1-5

One day the disciples asked Jesus, "Who will be the greatest in God's kingdom?" Jesus looked around and saw a child peeking out from behind the people in the crowd. He called the child over and pulled him gently into His arms.

"I promise you this," said Jesus to the disciples. "If you don't change and become like this child, you will never get into the kingdom of heaven. A child accepts God with a pure and humble heart. If you do this, you will be the greatest in God's kingdom. When you welcome one of these children, you welcome Me."

I Am with You

Matthew 18:15-20

Jesus said, "If your friend sins against you, go and speak with that person. But do it just between the two of you. If that person listens, you have won back your friend. If that person refuses to listen, take along one or two others and speak with that person again. If the person still does not hear what you say, go to the congregation.

I promise you that whenever you pray with others and your hearts are one, My Father in heaven will answer your prayer. And whenever two or three of you come together in My name, I am there with you."

The Rich Young Man

Matthew 19:16-22

A rich man came to Jesus and asked, "Teacher, what good things must I do to get into heaven?" Jesus answered, "Only God is truly good. If you want to enter into heaven, obey God's words."

Then the man asked, "Which words should I obey?" Jesus answered, "The commandments: Do not murder. Be faithful in marriage. Do not steal. Do not tell lies. Respect your parents. And love others as you do yourself!"

The man nodded. "Yes, Jesus. I have obeyed all of these rules," he said. "What else should I do?" Jesus replied, "If you want to do more, go beyond simply obeying the rules. Sell the things you own, and give to those who do not have anything. Then come and be My follower, and you will be on the right path."

When the young man heard this, he was sad because he was very rich.

The Five Careless Bridesmaids

Matthew 25:1-13

Jesus told this story about preparing for God's kingdom: "A big wedding party was about to happen. Ten girls took oil lamps to light the darkness while they waited for the groom to arrive and invite them in to the party. Five of the girls were wise and brought extra oil. Five of the girls were foolish and did not. The girls waited and waited. Soon they became drowsy and fell asleep. Then someone

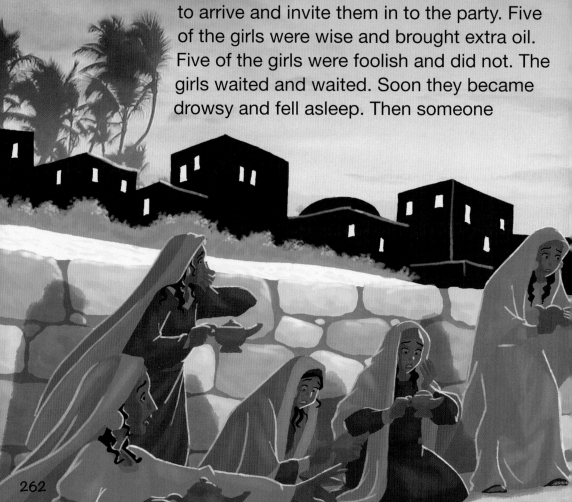

shouted, 'The groom is on his way! Let's go meet him!'

"The five girls who did not have extra oil cried out, 'We are out of oil! Share some with us.' But the other five answered, 'You must go buy your own.' While they were gone to buy oil, the groom came. The five that were ready went with him to the party, and the doors were shut.

"My friends," Jesus said, "do not be like the five girls who were not prepared. The doors of heaven will not be open to you unless you are ready for God at any moment."

The Big Parade

Luke 19:28-38

Jesus was nearing Jerusalem. He sent two of His disciples ahead of Him. "Go into the next village," He instructed them. "There you'll see a donkey tied to a pole. Untie the donkey, and bring it to Me. If anyone asks why you are taking it, tell them the Lord needs it."

The disciples went and found the donkey Jesus was talking about. As they began to untie it, the owner of the donkey snapped at them. "What do you think you're doing?" But the man let them go when they told him the Lord needed it. They brought the donkey to Jesus, and He climbed on its back. Then He rode down the Mount of Olives toward Jerusalem.

The people were waiting for Him down below. They laid their coats on the ground to make a path for Jesus and waved large palm branches. They said, "Blessed is the Lord our King! May there be peace and glory in the highest heaven!"

265

A New Command

John 13:31-35

Jesus told His disciples, "I will have to leave you all soon. You will look for Me, but I won't be there. God is going to bring glory to His Son! My time has come to go and be with My Father. But I will leave you with a new command. My command is that you love each other just as I have loved you. If you do as I say, then the world will know that you are truly My followers."

The Leaders Shall Serve

Luke 22:14, 24-30

Jesus and His disciples sat down to eat the Passover meal. While they were eating, one of them asked, "Who is the greatest among God's people?" All the disciples had a different opinion. They began to argue.

Jesus told them, "Some of you may think a ruler is the greatest because he orders people around. But don't be like that. The greatest person is the one who serves others. I have been a servant to you.

"Soon I will be gone. If you continue to serve, you will rule with Me in My kingdom. Each of you will have a throne, and you will eat and drink at My table."

269

The Lord's Supper

Mark 14:18-24

Jesus told His disciples, "One of you eating with Me is going to betray Me." The disciples hung their heads. They felt sad.

"Surely You don't mean me?" each of them asked Jesus. "I would never do a thing like that," each of them said. Jesus told them, "I will die and go to the Father. But it will be terrible for the man who betrays Me. He will wish he had never been born." Then Jesus picked up the loaf of bread from the table. He gave thanks and then broke the bread in two. "Take this bread and eat it," He told them. "It is My body broken for you." Then Jesus took the cup of wine, gave thanks, and passed it around. "Take this wine and drink it. It is My blood poured out for many. My blood seals the new covenant." So the disciples ate and drank. Jesus told them, "I will give up My body for you so that your sins may be forgiven."

Peter Will Deny Jesus

Mark 14:26-31

When the disciples had finished their meal, they sang a hymn and left the place. They went to the Mount of Olives. While they were there, Jesus told them, "I will die, and each one of you will turn your back on Me. You will be scattered and lost like sheep. But this won't be the end. I will come back and lead you again."

"Lord," Peter said. "Even if the others turn their backs on You, I never will."

But Jesus knew the truth. He said, "You will reject Me this very night. Before the rooster crows, three times you will say that you don't know Me."

Peter didn't believe Him. "No, I will never do that," he replied. All the other disciples said the same thing.

A Home in Heaven

John 14:1-7

The disciples felt sad, and Jesus could see it in their faces, so He told them, "Don't worry! Have faith in God, and have faith in Me. It's true that I cannot stay with you. But there are many rooms in God's house. I am going ahead of you to prepare a place where we can be together. I wouldn't tell you this if it weren't true."

"Lord," the disciple Thomas replied, "we don't know where You're going. How can we follow You if we don't know the way?"

Jesus told him, "I am the way, the truth, and the life! The only way to My Father is through Me."

Jesus Prays for His Followers

John 17:1-18:1

After Jesus finished speaking with His disciples, He went off to pray by Himself. "Father, You have given Me many followers. They have believed in Me. They know that I am Your Son. Now I am coming home to You, but help My followers who are still in the world. Protect them by Your power, and bring them closer to Your Word. Keep them safe. I also pray for those who will believe in Me through their message. Let them be as one people the way the Father and Son are one that the world may believe that You have sent Me."

Jesus finished His prayer and went with His disciples into the garden of Gethsemane.

The Disciples Fall Asleep

Mark 14:33-42

Jesus felt sad and troubled. He knew He was going to die soon. "Will you stay awake and pray with Me?" He asked His disciples. Then He walked a few steps away and knelt in the grass. "Abba, Father! You can do all things. Take this cup of suffering away from Me. But do what You want, not what I want."

Jesus went back to His disciples. They had all fallen asleep. He said to Peter, "Can't you stay awake with Me for one hour?" But they couldn't keep their eyes open. They just mumbled and fell asleep again after Jesus left to pray.

One last time, He went back to the disciples. "Wake up! It's time for Me to be taken away from you. The one who has betrayed Me is already coming this way into the garden."

Betrayed with a Kiss

John 18:2-8; Matthew 26:48-49

Judas Iscariot, one of the disciples, told the soldiers where they could find Jesus. "He will be in the garden with the other disciples, and you will know who Jesus is because I'll give Him a kiss on the cheek." The plan was settled. They lit their torches and carried their weapons. Then they followed Judas to the garden of Gethsemane.

Jesus saw them coming. "Who are you looking for?" He asked them.

"We've come to arrest Jesus," they answered.

"I am Jesus," He said. When Jesus said this, the soldiers drew back and fell to the ground. So Jesus asked them again, "Who are you looking for?"

"We've come for Jesus," they answered.

"I am the one you want, so if you are seeking Me, let My disciples go," Jesus said. Then Judas walked up to Jesus and kissed Him on the cheek. The soldiers grabbed Jesus and arrested Him.

Pilate Tries to Free Jesus

John 18:28-40

Jesus was taken to the chief priest's house, where He was charged with blasphemy because He said He was the Son of God. Then He was taken to Pilate's palace to be tried. Pilate was the Roman governor. There was a large crowd gathered outside Pilate's palace. Pilate came out and asked what the problem was. When he heard it was a charge of blasphemy he said, "Since it is about your religion, why don't you punish Him?"

But the people cried back, "It's against the law for us to crucify Him. We need you to do it! He also calls Himself a king." So Pilate went back inside and asked Jesus, "Are You the King of the Jews? The people are saying that You call Yourself a king," Pilate said. "My kingdom does not belong to this world," Jesus replied. "If it did, My servants would have fought to keep Me from being given over to the Jewish leaders." "So," Pilate said, "You admit to being a king!"

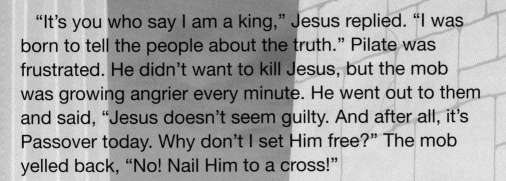

"It's you who say I am a king," Jesus replied. "I was born to tell the people about the truth." Pilate was frustrated. He didn't want to kill Jesus, but the mob was growing angrier every minute. He went out to them and said, "Jesus doesn't seem guilty. And after all, it's Passover today. Why don't I set Him free?" The mob yelled back, "No! Nail Him to a cross!"

Jesus Is Sentenced to Death

John 19:1-16

Pilate tried to calm the mob. But people kept shouting because the priests urged them to. "Tie Jesus up, and we'll beat Him," Pilate told his soldiers. "That should satisfy the people." So they beat Jesus and put a crown of thorns on

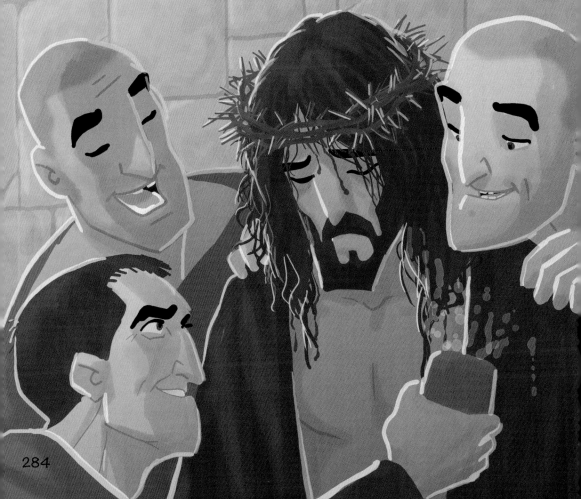

His head, but the people were not satisfied. "Crucify Him! Crucify Him!" they chanted.

Pilate went over to Jesus. "Where do You come from?" he asked. But Jesus was silent. "Why don't You answer me? Don't You know I have the power to free You?"

Jesus lifted His wearied head and replied, "Only God has the power to free Me. Without His permission, you couldn't do anything at all to Me."

Pilate asked the mob again, "So, you really want me to kill your king?"

"He's not our king," the people yelled back. "Only the emperor is king." Pilate finally gave in and handed Jesus over to be killed.

The Weeping Women

Luke 23:26-31

The soldiers made Jesus carry His own cross. Then they led Him up a hill. The mob of people followed behind Him. Most of them just wanted to see what was going on. But some of Jesus' loyal followers were there. A group of women who loved Jesus followed closely behind Him, weeping the whole way. Finally Jesus turned around and spoke to them. "Dear women, don't cry for Me! Cry for yourselves and for your children. Someday God will judge His people. Then everyone will say to the mountains, 'Fall on us!' and call out to the hills, 'Hide us!' But they will have no place to hide from God."

Jesus Is Nailed to a Cross

Luke 23:32-38

They nailed Jesus to a cross. There was a sign above His head that read, "The King of the Jews." The soldiers also crucified two criminals alongside Jesus. The people watched from down below. Some of them made fun of Jesus and

called Him names. "Why can't You save Yourself?" the soldiers taunted Him. "We thought You were the Lord!" Then they gambled for His clothes.

While Jesus was on the cross, He prayed, "Forgive these people, Father! They don't know what they're doing."

Jesus Dies

Luke 23:39-44; John 19:28-30

One of the criminals who was being crucified shouted insults to Jesus: "Aren't You the Lord? Save Yourself and save us!"

But the other criminal told him, "Don't You fear God? We are punished for doing wrong. But Jesus is truly innocent." Then he said to Jesus, "Remember me when You come to Your kingdom."

Jesus replied, "I promise that today you will be with Me in Paradise." Just then a cloud blocked the sun, and the sky turned dark. Jesus knew His time was almost done. "I'm thirsty!" He said. So someone soaked a sponge with vinegar. They tied it to a long plant stem and lifted it to Jesus' mouth. Then He said, "It is finished!" And He bowed His head and died.

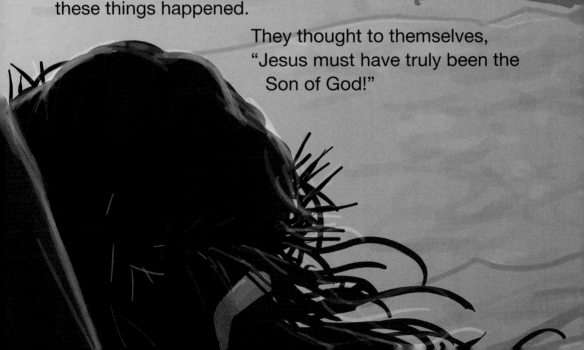

The Earth Trembles

Matthew 27:51-54

The moment Jesus died, the heavy curtain in Jerusalem's temple was torn in two, from top to bottom, the earth shook, rocks split apart and graves opened. The bodies of many godly men and women who had died were raised from the dead. (Later, after Jesus rose to life again, they would walk into Jerusalem and appear to many people.) Many of the soldiers and leaders of Israel were scared when all these things happened.

They thought to themselves, "Jesus must have truly been the Son of God!"

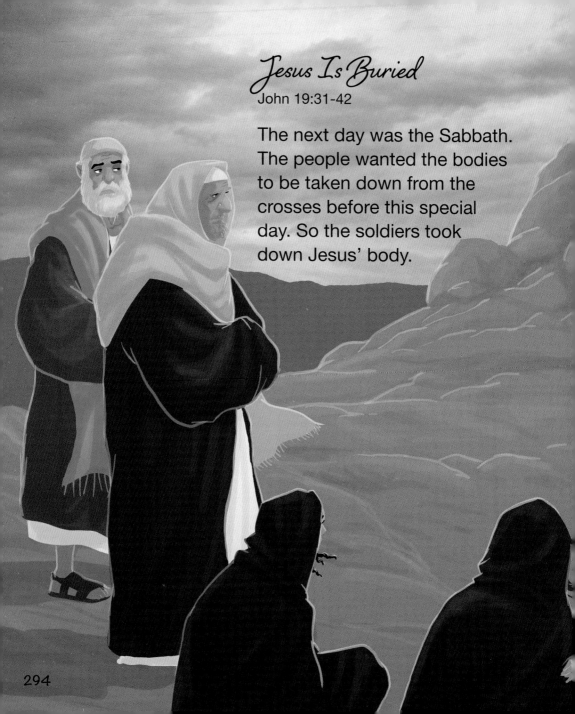

Jesus Is Buried

John 19:31-42

The next day was the Sabbath. The people wanted the bodies to be taken down from the crosses before this special day. So the soldiers took down Jesus' body.

But two of Jesus' secret followers named Joseph of
Arimathea and Nicodemus got permission from Pilate to
bury Jesus. They had bought spiced ointment, a mixture of
myrrh and aloe, and white linen to embalm the body. Then
they put Him in a tomb that had been cut out in the rocks.
They rolled a heavy stone over the entrance and left.

MARY MAGDALENE

- Mentioned in: Matthew, Mark, Luke, and John
- Meaning of name: Magdalene refers to where Mary was from, Magdala.
- She lived in: Magdala, on the coast of Galilee, Israel

Milestones:

Mary was possessed by seven demons that controlled her mind, but even so, she was a good woman. Jesus cast out her demons, and Mary became a godly woman, devoted to Jesus. She was the last person at the cross when Jesus died and the first at His tomb when He arose. Mary was one of the most devoted women in the Bible.

Some of Jesus' disciples betrayed Him, but Mary, a dedicated follower of Jesus, never did. Have you ever known someone whom you could count on no matter what? How does it make you feel to know you can always rely on them?

The angel said to the women, "Do not be afraid, for I know that you are looking for Jesus, who was crucified. He is not here; he has risen, just as he said. Come and see the place where he lay."
Matthew 28:5-6

Jesus Has Risen

Matthew 28:1-10

Mary Magdalene went to visit
Jesus' tomb with the other Mary.
But as soon as they arrived, an
earthquake rumbled and shook
the ground. Two soldiers, who
were guarding Jesus' tomb, were so
frightened that they both fainted. Then
an angel of the Lord came down from
heaven and rolled the heavy round stone
away from the tomb. His clothes were bright
white, and his face was shining. "Don't be
afraid," the angel told the women. "I know
you've come to be with Jesus. But He isn't here.
God has raised Him to life!"

The women were speechless. They started
running back to town—full of joy and excitement.
They couldn't wait to tell the disciples what the angel
had said. While they were on their way, Jesus suddenly
met them. The women came up to Jesus, took hold of
His feet, and worshiped Him. "Don't be afraid," He said
with a smile, "Go and tell My disciples that I will meet them
in Galilee."

The Empty Tomb
John 20:2-10

Mary Magdalene found Simon Peter and said, "The tomb is empty! Jesus is no longer there!" Peter had to see it with his own eyes. He immediately got up and ran toward the tomb. Another disciple went with him and got there before Peter. But he didn't go inside. So Peter went in first. Jesus wasn't there! But he saw the linen that had been wrapped around Jesus' body. The cloth that had covered Jesus' head lay nicely folded by itself. The other disciple came inside too. He saw and believed. The two of them went back to tell the other disciples.

Jesus Returns to God

Acts 1:3-11

Jesus stayed with His disciples forty days after He had risen from the grave.

He spoke of the Kingdom of God and said, "John baptized you with water, but in a few days, you will be baptized with the Holy Spirit."

The disciples had many questions, but Jesus said, "Do not worry. the Holy Spirit will come to you. Then you will receive power. You will be My witnesses—in Jerusalem, in all of Judea, in Samaria, and in every part of the world." After He said this, Jesus rose up in the sky to heaven as they watched.

His disciples stood staring up at the sky where Jesus had disappeared into the clouds when two strangers in white stood beside them and asked, "Why do you stand here? You saw Jesus go up into heaven, but He will return in the same way you saw Him leave."